Practice*Planners*

Arthur E. Jongsma, Jr., Series Editor

Helping therapists help their clients...

Treatment Planners cover all the necessary elements for developing formal treatment plans, including detailed problem definitions, long-term goals, short-term objectives, therapeutic interventions, and DSM-IV™ diagnoses.

The **Complete Treatment and Homework Planners** series of books combines our bestselling *Treatment Planners* and *Homework Planners* into one easy-to-use, all-in-one resource for mental health professionals treating clients suffering from the most commonly diagnosed disorders.

Over 500,000 Practice*Planners*® sold ...

 **WILEY**

Practice *Planners*®

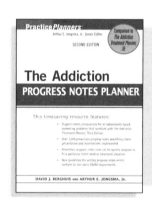

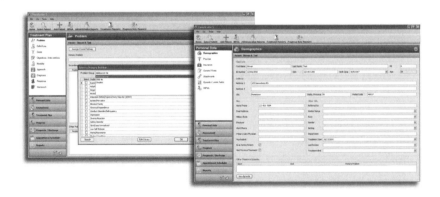

WILEY CONTINUING EDUCATION

FOR BEHAVIORAL HEALTH PROFESSIONALS

BOOK-BASED ONLINE LEARNING

Earn Accredited Continuing Education Online and On Time

NOW YOU CAN EARN CONTINUING EDUCATION CREDITS THROUGH OUR NEW BOOK-BASED, ONLINE EDUCATION PARTNERSHIP.

Our publications provide high quality continuing education to meet the licensing renewal needs of busy professionals like yourself. Best of all, you can complete this continuing education when and where you choose! Simply read the book, take the online test associated with the book and as soon as you have passed the test and completed the evaluation, you can print out your CE credit certificate— a valuable benefit for those facing imminent license renewal deadlines.

Clinical book content and the associated assessments meet the requirements of many state licensing boards and national accreditation bodies such as:

■ American Psychological Association
■ Association of Social Work Boards
■ National Board of Certified Counselors
■ National Association of Alcohol and Drug Abuse Counselors
■ American Nurses Credentialing Center

Topics covered include:

■ Addiction and Recovery
■ Forensic Psychology
■ Psychological Assessment
■ School Psychology
■ Therapy and Counseling

Each available book has a companion online course that consists of the Learning Objectives, post-test and course evaluation, so you can take them from anywhere you have Internet access. Likewise, you can take these courses at your own pace, any time of the day or night—whenever you have the time.

IT'S EASY TO GET STARTED!
Visit us online today at
www.wiley.com/go/ceuLearn
to find out how.

WILEY

Now you know.

wiley.com

*Wiley CE is provided through our partnership with Essential Learning.

Parenting Skills
Homework Planner

PRACTICE*PLANNERS*® SERIES

Treatment Planners

The Complete Adult Psychotherapy Treatment Planner, 3e
The Child Psychotherapy Treatment Planner, 3e
The Adolescent Psychotherapy Treatment Planner, 3e
The Addiction Treatment Planner, 2e
The Continuum of Care Treatment Planner
The Couples Psychotherapy Treatment Planner
The Employee Assistance Treatment Planner
The Pastoral Counseling Treatment Planner
The Older Adult Psychotherapy Treatment Planner
The Behavioral Medicine Treatment Planner
The Group Therapy Treatment Planner, 2e
The Gay and Lesbian Psychotherapy Treatment Planner
The Family Therapy Treatment Planner
The Severe and Persistent Mental Illness Treatment Planner
The Mental Retardation and Development Disability Treatment Planner
The Social Work and Human Services Treatment Planner
The Crisis Counseling and Traumatic Events Treatment Planner
The Personality Disorders Treatment Planner
The Rehabilitation Psychology Treatment Planner
The Special Education Treatment Planner
The Juvenile Justice and Residential Care Treatment Planner
The School Counseling and School Social Work Treatment Planner
The Sexual Abuse Victim and Sexual Offender Treatment Planner
The Probation and Parole Treatment Planner
The Psychopharmacology Treatment Planner
The Speech-Language Pathology Treatment Planner
The Suicide and Homicide Risk Assessment & Prevention Treatment Planner
The College Student Counseling Treatment Planner
The Parenting Skills Treatment Planner
The Early Childhood Intervention Treatment Planner

Progress Notes Planners

The Child Psychotherapy Progress Notes Planner, 2e
The Adolescent Psychotherapy Progress Notes Planner, 2e
The Adult Psychotherapy Progress Notes Planner, 2e
The Addiction Progress Notes Planner
The Severe and Persistent Mental Illness Progress Notes Planner
The Couples Psychotherapy Progress Notes Planner
The Family Therapy Progress Notes Planner

Homework Planners

Brief Therapy Homework Planner
Brief Couples Therapy Homework Planner
Brief Adolescent Therapy Homework Planner
Brief Child Therapy Homework Planner
Brief Employee Assistance Homework Planner
Brief Family Therapy Homework Planner
Grief Counseling Homework Planner
Group Therapy Homework Planner
Divorce Counseling Homework Planner
School Counseling and School Social Work Homework Planner
Child Therapy Activity and Homework Planner
Addiction Treatment Homework Planner, 2e
Adolescent Psychotherapy Homework Planner II
Adult Psychotherapy Homework Planner
Parenting Skills Homework Planner

Client Education Handout Planners

Adult Client Education Handout Planner
Child and Adolescent Client Education Handout Planner
Couples and Family Client Education Handout Planner

Complete Planners

The Complete Depression Treatment and Homework Planner
The Complete Anxiety Treatment and Homework Planner

PracticePlanners®

Arthur E. Jongsma, Jr., Series Editor

Parenting Skills
Homework Planner

Sarah Edison Knapp

WILEY

John Wiley & Sons, Inc.

Note about Photocopy Rights

The publisher grants purchasers permission to reproduce handouts from this book for professional use with their clients.

ISBN-13: 978-0-471-48182-9
ISBN-10: 0-471-48182-3

Printed in the United States of America.

10 9 8 7 6 5 4

To parents throughout the world
who are striving to safely and successfully
parent their children.

CONTENTS

PRACTICE*PLANNERS*® SERIES PREFACE

The practice of psychotherapy has a dimension that did not exist 30, 20, or even 15 years ago—accountability. Treatment programs, public agencies, clinics, and even group and solo practitioners must now justify the treatment of patients to outside review entities that control the payment of fees. This development has resulted in an explosion of paperwork.

Clinicians must now document what has been done in treatment, what is planned for the future, and what the anticipated outcomes of the interventions are. The books and software in this Practice*Planners*® series are designed to help practitioners fulfill these documentation requirements efficiently and professionally.

The Practice*Planners*® series is growing rapidly. It now includes not only the original *Complete Adult Psychotherapy Treatment Planner,* third edition, *The Child Psychotherapy Treatment Planner,* third edition, and *The Adolescent Psychotherapy Treatment Planner,* third edition, but also Treatment Planners targeted to specialty areas of practice, including: addictions, juvenile justice/residential care, couples therapy, employee assistance, behavioral medicine, therapy with older adults, pastoral counseling, family therapy, group therapy, neuropsychology, therapy with gays and lesbians, special education, school counseling, probation and parole, therapy with sexual abuse victims and offenders, and more.

Several of the Treatment Planner books now have companion Progress Notes Planners (e.g., Adult, Adolescent, Child, Addictions, Severe and Persistent Mental Illness, Couples, Family). More of these planners that provide a menu of progress statements that elaborate on the client's symptom presentation and the provider's therapeutic intervention are in production. Each Progress Notes Planner statement is directly integrated with "Behavioral Definitions" and "Therapeutic Interventions" items from the companion Treatment Planner.

The list of therapeutic Homework Planners is also growing from the original Brief Therapy Homework for Adults to Adolescent, Child, Couples, Group, Family, Addictions, Divorce, Grief, Employee Assistance, School Counseling/School Social Work Homework Planners, and Parenting Skills. Each of these books can be used alone or in conjunction with their companion Treatment Planner. Homework assignments are designed around each presenting problem (e.g., Anxiety, Depression, Chemical Dependence, Anger Management, Panic, Eating Disorders) that is the focus of a chapter in its corresponding Treatment Planner.

Client Education Handout Planners, a new branch in the series, provides brochures and handouts to help educate and inform adult, child, adolescent, couples, and family clients on a myriad of mental health issues, as well as life skills techniques. The list of presenting problems for which information is provided mirrors the list of presenting problems in the Treatment Planner of the title similar to that of the Handout Planner. Thus, the problems for which educational material is provided in the *Child and Adolescent Client Education Handout Planner* reflect the presenting problems listed in *The Child Psychotherapy Treatment Planner* and *The Adolescent Psychotherapy Treatment Planner*. Handouts are included on CD-ROMs for easy printing and are ideal for use in waiting rooms, at presentations, as newsletters, or as information for clients struggling with mental illness issues.

In addition, the series also includes Thera*Scribe*®, the latest version of the popular software for treatment planning and clinical record-keeping. Thera*Scribe*® allows the user to import the data from any of the Treatment Planner, Progress Notes Planner, or Homework Planner books into the software's expandable database. Then the point-and-click method can create a detailed, neatly organized, individualized, and customized treatment plan along with optional integrated progress notes and homework assignments.

Adjunctive books, such as *The Psychotherapy Documentation Primer,* and *Clinical, Forensic, Child, Couples and Family, Continuum of Care,* and *Chemical Dependence Documentation Sourcebook* contain forms and resources to aid the mental health practice management. The goal of the series is to provide practitioners with the resources they need in order to provide high-quality care in the era of accountability—or, to put it simply, we seek to help you spend more time on patients, and less time on paperwork.

ARTHUR E. JONGSMA, JR.
Grand Rapids, Michigan

ACKNOWLEDGMENTS

Many thanks to Arthur Jongsma, the series editor and coauthor of the Treatment Planners, which have helped hundreds of thousands of therapists in numerous treatment settings. *The Parenting Skills Treatment Planner* and the *Parenting Skills Homework Planner* are a much needed addition to the planner series and are now available due to his foresight, dedication, and diligence. I have often wished that I had these useful therapeutic guides while I was working with children and their parents in the school setting and as a parent trainer. Thanks to Peggy Alexander, vice president and publisher, and her staff at John Wiley & Sons for their support and encouragement. Finally, thank you to my own children, Michael Knapp Jr. and Heather Werkemam, my sisters, Judith Forker and Ann Walz, and my amazing extended family members, for their love, encouragement, good humor, and insight, which helped me understand and appreciate the role of the family in supporting and celebrating all personal efforts. You made it all worthwhile.

INTRODUCTION

Family counselors and therapists are seeing more and more families with varied and difficult issues to manage and overcome. The role of the family therapist is to assist the parents, children, and other family members in solving the problems that are interfering with the child's successful adjustment within the family, at school, and to life in general. Homework assignments and activities used to reinforce and supplement the counseling sessions help the parents and the child invest in the therapeutic process and take responsibility for the effort necessary to reach the treatment goals.

The assignments provided in this planner are designed to enhance the therapeutic interventions described in *The Parenting Skills Treatment Planner* (Knapp & Jongsma, 2004). The activities will help parents evaluate family problems, utilize positive strategies of discipline that promote responsible behavior, and build positive relationships with their children. These exercises can be assigned as part of the counseling session or as homework between sessions to reinforce the insights and information processed during the individual or group sessions.

Homework activities speed up the attainment of therapeutic goals. Through completion of the assignment the parents become increasingly aware of the process of problem solving and the behavioral changes necessary to reach the therapeutic goals. The activities help the parents and the child to clarify their issues of conflict and detrimental behavior patterns. They empower the family members to become actively involved in attaining social/emotional health. The insight gained as a result of the completed homework can be discussed during subsequent counseling sessions and used as a basis for more productive, successful behavior and thought patterns.

During my 25 years as a social worker in the schools and as a parenting class facilitator, I used numerous written and interactive activities to enhance the therapeutic process with parents and their children of all ages and with varied social-emotional problems. Creating these activities was labor intensive and time consuming. The *Parenting Skills Homework Planner* provides 60 homework activities ready to copy and use with parents and their children. This book will eliminate the hours spent preparing activities for families with a wide range of therapeutic issues.

USING THIS HOMEWORK PLANNER WITH FAMILIES

Homework activities will help the parents and the child take the therapeutic process seriously and recognize their essential part in creating change. All of the activities are designed to be interesting as well as helpful in resolving therapeutic issues. However, homework may have a negative connotation to parents who already feel overwhelmed by the demands of work and family obligations. For parents and children who are reluctant to complete additional assignments, it will be helpful to begin the homework activity during the counseling session and to spend time discussing how the assignment will be helpful in addressing the problem. Each exercise should be processed during the next session to reinforce the value of the activity and to acknowledge the family members' time and effort spent completing the homework. If the activity assignment has not has not been finished, time can be provided during the next session, and reasons for lack of completion can be discussed. This process will help the therapist understand more fully how the family deals with tasks, assignments, and obligations.

Many activities can be used as part of the counseling session and will facilitate dialogue on the particular issues being considered. The activities are designed to be completed by the parents individually or working together with their child.

ABOUT THE ASSIGNMENTS

There are one or more assignments that correlate directly with each treatment concern presented in *The Parenting Skills Treatment Planner*. These assignments are cited as part of the therapeutic interventions recommended for each identified problem in the Treatment Planner. Each activity begins with a Counselor's Overview that cites goals of the exercise, additional homework that may be applicable to the problem, additional problems the exercise may be useful for, and suggestions for using the exercise with the parents and the child. These assignments are ready to copy and use with the family. Each activity provides instructions for the parents and child; however, in most cases these instructions should be covered and clarified during the counseling session. Not all assignments will be applicable to all families. Professional judgment should be used in assigning the activities. Often, homework activities from other sections of the *Parenting Skills Homework Planner* will be applicable to the presenting problem. A cross-reference for additional assignments is provided in the "Alternate Assignments for Presenting Problems Appendix" at the end of the book. All of the assignments can be tailored to fit the individual circumstances and needs of the parents and the child by using the CD-ROM which accompanies the *Homework Planner*. The therapist should feel free to alter the activities to best suit the requirements of the family and the issues being addressed.

It is recommended that the therapist read through the entire book to become familiar with the activities that may be helpful to the parents and the child. If the parents are being seen for several sessions or for an extended period of time, the activities can be kept in a therapeutic journal or notebook for easy reference and review. The notebook will become a record of the progress made during the counseling process, and should be given to the parents upon termination of the sessions.

The activities in the *Parenting Skills Homework Planner* are designed to accompany the therapeutic counseling process and should not be used independently without the guidance of a family counselor or therapist.

SARAH EDISON KNAPP

Section I

ABUSIVE PARENTING

OUR FAMILY'S SECRET STORY

GOALS OF THE EXERCISE

1. Disclose the story of the child abuse using the process of journaling.
2. Identify the parents' thoughts and feelings connected with the child's abuse in a supportive, therapeutic environment.
3. Clarify how the abuse has affected all aspects of the family's life.
4. Identify support systems available to help the family deal with the ramifications of the abuse.
5. Prepare for dealing with the abuse and moving ahead with life.

ADDITIONAL HOMEWORK THAT MAY BE APPLICABLE TO VICTIMS OF CHILD ABUSE

ADDITIONAL PROBLEMS THIS EXERCISE MAY BE MOST USEFUL FOR

*   Grief/Loss
*   Divorce
*   Depression
*   Posttraumatic Stress Disorder (PTSD)
*   Suicide

SUGGESTIONS FOR USING THIS EXERCISE WITH PARENTS

Families who have experienced physical or sexual abuse may find it difficult to disclose their personal thoughts and feelings, even to a supportive therapist. The "Our Family's

Secret Story" activity encourages the parents to record their personal ideas privately, in writing, and then share them with the therapist during a counseling session. Journaling allows the parents to record their reactions before disclosing them. The activity lists 25 journal entry starters to help the parents describe the story of abuse in a sequential manner and to consider the most common and relevant aspects of abuse on the child.

OUR FAMILY'S SECRET STORY

Writing down thoughts and feelings can help sort out the many difficult, challenging, discouraging, or traumatic experiences connected to the history of abuse in the family and its effects upon you and your child. The feelings you experience as a result of any type of abuse are varied and sometimes extremely confusing. By writing down these reactions in a story format or in a personal journal you will begin to understand and make sense of what happened, how the abuse affected you, the child, and the family as a whole, and how you will manage the difficult experience and go on from here. Your written words will help you to express yourself more clearly during your counseling or therapy sessions, and to determine strategies for helping your child cope with the effects of abuse. Remember that your journal is private, and only you can decide whether to share your personal notes. However, therapy will be much more effective if you are willing to share your written thoughts and feelings with your family counselor.

This activity is just a beginning to help you establish the habit of journaling. If you journal regularly you will find that you understand yourself, your spouse, and your child more fully and become better prepared to deal with personal and family challenges. Complete the following starter sentences in order to tell your family's story. If you have additional thoughts and responses to record, use the back of the paper or additional notepaper to describe all of the important aspects of your story.

Answer a few of the following questions each week in order to prepare for your counseling session. You may answer the questions in order or decide which ones to complete each week. Try to find a quiet, peaceful place to do your journaling. After you have completed all of the questions, continue the journaling process by responding to questions developed by you and your counselor—or simply record a couple of paragraphs describing your personal experiences or feelings each day.

1. Describe the family environment before the abuse occurred (e.g., parent/child attachments, sibling relationships, social/emotional problems, discipline challenges, marital conflict).

   _____

   _____

   _____

   _____

   _____

2. Is there a previous history or intergenerational pattern of abuse in the family?

_____

_____

_____

_____

_____

3. Describe the effects of the abuse on the child.

_____

_____

_____

_____

_____

4. Describe the effects of the abuse on the child's siblings.

_____

_____

_____

_____

_____

5. Describe how the abuse has affected you.

_____

_____

_____

_____

_____

6. What was the child's relationship with the perpetrator before the abuse?

_____

_____

_____

_____

_____

7. When did the abuse first occur?

    _____

    _____

    _____

    _____

8. How long did the abuse go on?

    _____

    _____

    _____

    _____

9. Describe the abuse in your own words.

    _____

    _____

    _____

    _____

    _____

    _____

10. Describe your thoughts and actions during the time the abuse was occurring.

    _____

    _____

    _____

    _____

    _____

    _____

11. Describe your emotions, thoughts, and actions after the abuse was disclosed.

    _____

    _____

    _____

    _____

    _____

12. How was the abuse discovered?

_____

_____

_____

_____

_____

_____

13. How did the child feel about disclosing the abuse?

_____

_____

_____

_____

_____

_____

14. Who helped the child and other family members with the disclosure? (How did they help?)

_____

_____

_____

_____

_____

15. How did your family and friends react to the disclosure?

_____

_____

_____

_____

_____

_____

16. Do you think someone could have prevented or stopped the abuse earlier? (Describe who and how.)

_____

_____

_____

_____

_____

17. How have the family dynamics changed as a result of the disclosure of the abuse?

_____

_____

_____

_____

_____

18. What has happened to the perpetrator as a result of the abuse?

_____

_____

_____

_____

_____

19. Do you think this is an appropriate consequence for the perpetrator? (Describe what you think would be appropriate.)

_____

_____

_____

_____

_____

20. What would you like to say to the perpetrator now?

_____

_____

_____

_____

21. Who has helped the child and other family members to deal with the abuse?

_____

_____

_____

_____

22. Have you experienced feelings of guilt, regret, or remorse concerning the abuse? (Describe.)

_____

_____

_____

_____

23. What other types of help or support do you, the child, and other family members need?

_____

_____

_____

_____

_____

24. Describe what is needed to help the child and other family members move on and lead a happy and successful life.

_____

_____

_____

_____

_____

25. Describe the family environment five years from now.

_____

_____

_____

_____

_____

26. Additional questions, comments, or concerns I have regarding the abuse.

_____

_____

_____

_____

_____

_____

_____

_____

_____

_____

_____

_____

_____

_____

_____

_____

_____

_____

_____

_____

_____

_____

_____

_____

_____

_____

_____

_____

_____

_____

MEASURING OUR FEELINGS

GOALS OF THE EXERCISE

1. Identify negative feelings associated with the experience of child abuse.
2. Identify positive feelings experienced as recovery begins.
3. Measure the ebb and flow and the intensity of the feelings experienced.
4. Develop a sense of control over personal feelings and attitude.

ADDITIONAL HOMEWORK THAT MAY BE APPLICABLE TO VICTIMS OF CHILD ABUSE

•	Grief/Loss	Monitoring Our Reactions to Change and Loss	Page 184
		Grief and Loss Circle of Support	Page 188
•	Depression	Creating Positive Self-Talk	Page 130
		Managing Positive and Negative Relationships	Page 134
•	Posttraumatic Stress Disorder (PTSD)	Reframing Our Worries	Page 216
		Physical Receptors of Stress	Page 220

ADDITIONAL PROBLEMS THIS EXERCISE MAY BE MOST USEFUL FOR

- Grief/Loss
- Depression
- Posttraumatic Stress Disorder (PTSD)
- Suicide

SUGGESTIONS FOR USING THIS EXERCISE WITH VICTIMS OF ABUSE

Victims of child abuse often feel overwhelmed and lack a feeling of control over their feelings and their lives. The "Measuring Our Feelings" activity helps the affected family members identify both the positive and negative feelings experienced after the disclosure of the abuse and the intensity of these feelings as the weeks toward recovery progress. The parents and identified child are asked to select personal feelings directly related to the abuse from a provided list and to graph the intensity of these feelings during the days between counseling sessions. Each family member may follow the same process for positive feelings during the same time frame. The weekly feelings' graphs should be saved in a personal journal or notebook to track the ebb and flow of feelings as the parents and child learn to cope with the aftermath of the abuse.

This exercise is designed to help the parents and the identified child recognize that through counseling and acquiring strategies to cope with personal trauma, feelings and attitude become a matter of personal choice. The parents and child are instructed to determine, with the help of the counselor, whether appropriate progress toward acceptance and adjustment is being accomplished.

MEASURING OUR FEELINGS

Provided is a list of feelings commonly experienced by victims of child abuse and their family members. Look over the list and add any additional words that represent feelings you are aware of or often experience. Notice that the list contains a mixture of positive and negative feelings. Children who have been abused and their close family members continue to experience pleasant and positive feelings along with their unpleasant and negative feelings of distress and victimization. Highlight or circle the feelings you are dealing with as a direct result of the abuse.

abandoned	ecstatic	jealous	shamed
angry	embarrassed	lazy	shocked
anxious	enraged	left out	shy
ashamed	excited	lonely	smart
badgered	exhausted	lovestruck	smug
betrayed	foolish	loving	surprised
bored	frightened	mad	suspicious
calm	frustrated	mischievous	uneasy
cautious	guilty	neglected	upset
chippy	happy	nervous	uptight
confident	helpless	overwhelmed	victimized
confused	hopeful	proud	welcome
curious	hopeless	sad	worried
depressed	horrified	scared	_____
disappointed	hysterical	serene	_____
disgusted	important	serious	_____

It is normal for parents and the identified child to feel upset and extremely concerned after disclosing an abusive situation. However, these negative reactions tend to ebb and flow as you begin to deal with the abuse through counseling and the support of family members and friends. As the counseling and adjustment progress, you and your child will again experience an increased amount of positive feelings and a decreased intensity of negative feelings. Eventually, it will become a personal decision whether to dwell on the negative feelings resulting from the abusive experience or to choose to focus on the positive aspects of your lives and experience joy and happiness once again.

Underline (or highlight in a different color) the positive feelings you experience occasionally now and hope to enjoy more frequently in the future. Use the graphs to measure the intensity of your positive and negative feelings over a 1-week period of time. Compare the intensity of your positive and negative feelings from week to week to determine if your attitude and outlook are becoming more negative, remaining the same, or becoming more positive. Complete each graph individually and then compare the results with your counselor and each other.

Negative feelings I have experienced during the week of _____.

Record eight negative feelings you have experienced this week in the spaces provided at the bottom of the chart. Estimate the level of intensity for each feeling by shading in the spaces up to the appropriate level. 0 to 30 is within the mild range of intensity, 30 to 60 is in the moderate range, 60 to 80 is a high level of intensity, and 80 to 100 indicates that you are overwhelmed by the feeling.

100								
90								
80								
70								
60								
50								
40								
30								
20								
10								
0								
Feeling being measured								

Positive feelings I have experienced during the week of _____.

Record eight positive feelings you have experienced this week in the spaces provided at the bottom of the chart. Estimate the level of intensity for each feeling by shading in the spaces up to the appropriate level.

100								
90								
80								
70								
60								
50								
40								
30								
20								
10								
0								
Feeling being measured								

Section II

ATTENTION-DEFICIT/HYPERACTIVITY DISORDER (ADHD)

ADHD ACCOMMODATIONS REQUEST FORM

GOALS OF THE EXERCISE

1. Identify factors that contribute to or detract from the child's ability to focus and concentrate.
2. Determine various accommodations that will help the child succeed socially and academically.
3. Improve the child's ability to remain on task during various activities and assignments.
4. Collaborate with the child's teachers, coaches, and mentors to improve the child's level of participation in various activities.

ADDITIONAL HOMEWORK THAT MAY BE APPLICABLE
MANAGING THE SYMPTOMS OF ADHD

- Strategies for Preschoolers (Ages Birth to 6)   Helping My Child Develop Responsible Behavior   Page 305
- Strategies for Elementary Children (Ages 7 to 12)   Record of Reinforced Behavior   Page 319
- School Adjustment Difficulties   Organizing for the School Day   Page 248

ADDITIONAL PROBLEMS THIS EXERCISE MAY BE MOST USEFUL FOR

- Strategies for Preschoolers
- Strategies for Elementary Children
- Strategies for Adolescents
- School Adjustment Difficulties

SUGGESTIONS FOR USING THIS EXERCISE WITH PARENTS

Accommodations, special programs, and support strategies can make the difference between a child with ADHD finding success and social adjustment—at home, in school, and during extracurricular activities. Section 504 of the Rehabilitation Act of 1973 requires that schools provide accommodations for children who have a qualifying physical or mental disability, including ADHD. However, parents often need to request that their child be considered for appropriate services. Both the parents and the child need to advocate for the specific accommodations required by the child in special circumstances. The ADHD Accommodations Request Form activity directs the parents and the child to identify factors that contribute to or detract from the child's ability to concentrate, follow directions, and complete assignments and to determine various accommodations that will help the child succeed socially and academically.

ADHD ACCOMMODATIONS REQUEST FORM

Child's Name: _____

DOB: _____

Parents' Names: _____   _____

Find a comfortable, distraction-free place to meet with your child and brainstorm a list of accommodations, programs, and support strategies that would facilitate the management of the child's ADHD symptoms. A separate list should be created for various problematic environments (e.g., school, home, church, sports activities, social events).

The rules for brainstorming are:

1. Each person actively participates in the process.

2. All ideas are acceptable and recorded in writing.

3. Select the most useful ideas from the recorded list.

A list of accommodations is provided below. Adapt any of these examples to the specific setting and the special needs of the child. Then create a final list of accommodations to present to the adult in charge of each activity or event. Be open-minded and flexible when negotiating for special considerations with the child's teacher, coach, or mentor. Remember that necessary accommodations can greatly enhance the child's ability to function successfully; however, unneeded accommodations can lead to dependency and lack of personal growth. Therefore, only necessary accommodations should be implemented, with the goal of encouraging the ADHD child to function as independently and responsibly as possible.

Typical accommodations to enhance successful participation:

1. Give class instructions from a specific spot in the classroom.

2. Seat the child near the instruction center.

3. Alert the child in advance of any changes in routine.

4. Maintain a consistent, predictable schedule.

5. Break assignments and instructions into short, sequential steps.

6. Test verbally and/or shorten tests.

7. Individualize homework assignments.

8. Identify and frequently verbalize the child's strengths.

9. Individualize expectations for problematic subject areas.

10. Provide a quiet study area.

11. Provide technological assistance (e.g., recorded books, earphones, taped lectures, calculator, word processor).

12. Help the child organize the learning environment and monitor frequently.

13. Establish immediate consequences for unacceptable behavior.

14. Allow for controlled movement (e.g., permit stretch breaks, encourage seat isometrics, seat at round table, assign two seats, use work breaks).

15. Maintain frequent physical proximity.

16. Encourage the child to use a personal planner and to keep "to do" lists.

17. Avoid embarrassment or put-downs of student.

18. Correct unacceptable behavior privately.

19. Provide school counseling and support groups.

20. Teach study and organizational skills.

21. Encourage peer support, friendship, and empathy.

22. Keep expectations realistic.

Additional ideas from our brainstorming session:

1. _____

2. _____

3. _____

4. _____

5. _____

6. _____

7. _____

8. _____

9. _____

10. _____

11. _____

12. _____

13. _____

14. _____

15. _____

Create a personalized list of useful accommodations for each problematic setting (e.g., school, church, family activities, social situations, sports).

Setting: _____

Useful accommodations:

1. _____

2. _____

3. _____

4. _____

5. _____

6. _____

7. _____

8. _____

Setting: _____

Useful accommodations:

1. _____

2. _____

3. _____

4. _____

5. _____

6. _____

7. _____

8. _____

Setting: _____

Useful accommodations:

1. _____
2. _____
3. _____
4. _____
5. _____
6. _____
7. _____
8. _____

Setting: _____

Useful accommodations:

1. _____
2. _____
3. _____
4. _____
5. _____
6. _____
7. _____
8. _____

FAMILY PROBLEM RESOLUTION WORKSHEET

GOALS OF THE EXERCISE

1. Identify and define family problems related to coping with ADHD.
2. Prioritize the ADHD-related problems from most to least troublesome.
3. Develop a strategy for resolving the identified problems one at a time.
4. Utilize family cooperation and collaboration to resolve problems.

ADDITIONAL HOMEWORK THAT MAY BE APPLICABLE TO PROBLEM RESOLUTION

• Strategies for Preschoolers (Ages Birth to 6)	Helping My Child Develop Responsible Behavior	Page 305
• Strategies for Children (Ages 7 to 12)	Problem-solving Worksheet	Page 323
• Children with Physical Challenges	Working Together to Create a Plan	Page 102

ADDITIONAL PROBLEMS THIS EXERCISE MAY BE MOST USEFUL FOR

- Strategies for Preschoolers
- Strategies for Children
- Strategies for Teenagers
- Children with Physical Challenges

SUGGESTIONS FOR USING THIS EXERCISE WITH PARENTS

Parents and their children coping with ADHD and other child-management concerns often feel inadequate or unprepared to solve problems and lack knowledge of an effective step-by-step process necessary to implement strategies for attaining a positive result. The "Family Problem Resolution Worksheet" assists family members in resolving problems by planning for a successful outcome. Family members are asked to brainstorm a list of challenges they are experiencing as a result of ADHD and to prioritize them in order of need to resolve. They are then directed to develop a plan for resolving these issues one at a time that includes a clear statement of the problem, possible interventions, and the designated family members responsible for the implementation of the plan. The results of the problem-solving efforts are recorded and saved for future reference and intervention if necessary.

FAMILY PROBLEM RESOLUTION WORKSHEET

Use this worksheet to identify problems your family is coping with as a result of the ADHD symptoms and behavior experienced by the child and other family members. Meet together as a family and brainstorm a list of 10 to 15 ADHD-related problems. Write these problems in the space provided and then work together to prioritize them from most to least troublesome.

Problems our family is coping with as a result of ADHD symptoms and behavior:

Example: Sherrie forgets to bring her books and assignments home from school.

Example: Jerome wastes time in the morning and is often late for school.

1. _____
2. _____
3. _____
4. _____
5. _____
6. _____
7. _____
8. _____
9. _____
10. _____
11. _____
12. _____
13. _____
14. _____
15. _____

Now choose a problem to be resolved. Select one of the easier or least troublesome issues first, to practice the problem-solving process and to gain some confidence and momentum before tackling the more difficult problems. Use the sheet provided to plan a solution to the selected problem, using the following process:

1. Define the problem by describing the specific behavior, when the behavior occurs, and who is negatively affected by the behavior.

2. Determine who is primarily responsible for correcting the behavior or solving the problem.

3. Brainstorm possible solutions to the problem and consider how each strategy might work.

4. Select one strategy or a combination of strategies to solve the problem.

5. Choose a second strategy as a backup plan in case the first strategy doesn't work out as well as hoped.

6. Identify family members who can support the problem owner in resolving the problem.

7. After giving the strategy time to work, record the results and indicate if the problem was solved.

8. Keep your worksheets in a family journal as a record of the family's cooperative problem-solving attempts and successes.

Example

Problem definition:

> Sherrie forgets to bring her books and assignments home from school. Her grades are dropping, and this concerns her mother and father. Often Sherrie and her parents argue about her forgetfulness and lack of responsibility.

Person responsible for solving the problem:

> Sherrie

Potential solutions:

Strategy	Possible Outcome
Maintain an assignment list	Sherrie gains homework awareness
Record assignments in a daily planner	Sherrie learns task management
Keep second set of books at home	Materials are available for homework
Parents access homework hotline	Parents monitor assignments
Teacher e-mails homework assignments	Reduction of homework arguments
Parents assign daily homework hour	Sherrie completes daily assignments

Strategies chosen for implementation:

Sherrie will maintain a daily assignment list and review the list nightly with her parents. Her parents will assign a nightly homework hour and help her organize how she will complete her assignments.

Backup strategies chosen for implementation:

Sherrie's parents will request that the teacher e-mail home daily assignments or will access the school's homework hotline.

People collaborating to solve the problem:

Sherrie, her parents, and possibly the teacher

Result:

Sherrie is beginning to record all of her daily assignments and discusses them with her parents prior to their participation in her nightly homework hour.

What will happen next:

Sherrie and her parents will meet again in two weeks to evaluate the results and plan for future interventions if necessary.

FAMILY PROBLEM RESOLUTION WORKSHEET

Problem definition:

_____

_____

Person responsible for solving the problem:

_____

Potential solutions:

Strategy	Possible Outcome
_____	_____
_____	_____
_____	_____
_____	_____
_____	_____
_____	_____

Strategies chosen for implementation:

_____

_____

_____

Backup strategies chosen for implementation:

_____

_____

_____

People collaborating to resolve the problem:

_____ _____

_____ _____

_____ _____

_____ _____

Result:

_____

_____

_____

What will happen next:

_____

_____

_____

People collaborating to resolve the problem: (Signatures)

                                        _____

                                        _____

                                        _____

                                        _____

                                        _____

                         Date: _____

Section III

ATTENTION-SEEKING BEHAVIOR

FAMILY JOB SUPPORT CHECKLIST

GOALS OF THE EXERCISE

1. Increase cooperative effort within the family.
2. Develop a family plan for mutual support and encouragement.
3. Improve willingness to ask for and receive help from family members.
4. Express appreciation for assistance received in completing household tasks.
5. Increase quality and efficiency in the completion of family chores and responsibilities.

ADDITIONAL HOMEWORK THAT MAY BE APPLICABLE TO FAMILY COOPERATION

• Bonding/Attachment Issues	Steps to Responsible Behavior	Page 60
• Character Development	Division of Family Labor	Page 86
• Children with Physical Challenges	Working Together to Create a Plan	Page 102
• Sibling Rivalry	Affirming Each Child's Uniqueness	Page 268

ADDITIONAL PROBLEMS THIS EXERCISE MAY BE MOST USEFUL FOR

- Academic Motivation
- Attention-Deficit/Hyperactivity Disorder (ADHD)
- Career Planning
- Learning Difficulties
- Responsible Behavior Training

SUGGESTIONS FOR USING THIS EXERCISE WITH FAMILIES

Help the parents and their children develop a plan for mutual support and encouragement in the completion of daily jobs, chores, and responsibilities. Suggest that the parents use the weekly family meeting forum to brainstorm a list of individual responsibilities that would benefit from sharing the workload with other family members (e.g., meal preparation, transportation to activities, homework, general cleaning, yard work). Then have each family member list several personal jobs and request assistance. Let family members volunteer to help, but encourage the equitable distribution of the jobs—keeping in mind each family member's maturity level and ability to perform each task.

Allow time during the next family meeting to evaluate the cooperative efforts, and to offer appreciation for the help and support that was extended—and to offer constructive feedback for efforts that were lacking or need improvement.

FAMILY JOB SUPPORT CHECKLIST

Some family jobs can be completed alone, while other jobs require the help and support of other family members. One great reason to live in a family is to benefit from a cooperative effort when tackling complicated or time-consuming jobs. The family meeting is a perfect time to brainstorm chores and jobs and request help when necessary. Use the following checklist to list the jobs each family member is responsible for that will need assistance from others. Identify who is available to help, and make sure that the workload is equitably distributed, with consideration given to age, maturity level, and ability to perform the required assistance. During the next family meeting allow time for the evaluation of the completed task and the expression of appreciation for the assistance received. Use the following evaluation form to assist in formulating specific and appreciative praise for the cooperative effort given and for constructive feedback for any areas that need improvement.

Jobs I Need Help Completing:	**Who Can Help:**
MOM	
Example: Preparing meals	Dad, siblings 1, 2, & 3
_____	_____
_____	_____
_____	_____
_____	_____
_____	_____
DAD	
Example: Yard work	Mom, siblings 1, 2, & 3
_____	_____
_____	_____
_____	_____
_____	_____
_____	_____

CHILD 1

Example: Cleaning room   Mom, Dad, sibling 2

_____   _____

_____   _____

_____   _____

_____   _____

_____   _____

_____   _____

CHILD 2

Example: Transportation to activities   Mom, Dad, sibling 3

_____   _____

_____   _____

_____   _____

_____   _____

_____   _____

_____   _____

CHILD 3

Example: Car maintenance   Mom, Dad, siblings 1 & 2

_____   _____

_____   _____

_____   _____

_____   _____

_____   _____

_____   _____

Job Evaluation Form

Name of job:

_____

Responsible person:

_____

Assistance given from:

_____

Evaluation of the job: Excellent ___ Good ___ Fair ___ Poor ___ Not completed ___

Constructive feedback: How this effort could have been even more productive:

_____

_____

_____

_____

_____

_____

_____

_____

_____

Specific and appreciative praise and encouragement for the effort given; I want to express my special thanks by saying:

_____

_____

_____

_____

_____

_____

_____

_____

_____

MY LOVE AND TRUST SUPPORT NETWORK

GOALS OF THE EXERCISE

1. Enhance feelings of support and security.
2. Recognize the existing support system.
3. View family, friends, and teachers as positive, loving, and helpful.
4. Strengthen relationships with significant others.

ADDITIONAL HOMEWORK THAT MAY BE APPLICABLE TO CHILDREN WITH ATTENTION SEEKING BEHAVIOR

- Posttraumatic Stress Disorder (PTSD)   Reframing Our Worries   Page 216
- Blended Family   Unique Roles in Our Blended Family   Page 53
- Grief/Loss   Grief and Loss Circle of Support   Page 188
- Sibling Rivalry   Affirming Each Child's Uniqueness   Page 268

ADDITIONAL PROBLEMS THIS EXERCISE MAY BE MOST USEFUL FOR

- Blended Family
- Depression
- Divorce
- Grief/Loss

SUGGESTIONS FOR USING THIS EXERCISE WITH FAMILIES

Children with low self-esteem and feelings of inadequacy frequently believe that no one loves or cares enough for them. Their needs for support and attention often appear insatiable, especially to their parents. Excessive attention-seeking behavior may develop which is based on false or skewed assumptions. Recognition of a personal support system enhances the child's self-esteem and reduces anxiety and feelings of helplessness and hopelessness. This exercise helps the child to increase awareness of those people that do care and are willing to help with personal concerns. The child will then discover the positive nature of relationships within the immediate and extended family, school, and community, and begin to view family members and other caring people from a more positive perspective. The parents are asked to assist the child in listing family members, relatives, friends, mentors, and role models who offer special support, encouragement, and unconditional love. Eight additional suggestions are listed, following the activity, for activities involving important people in the child's life.

INTRODUCTION TO THE PARENTS AND THE CHILD

Work together to identify several positive people in the child's life by writing their names in the spaces provided, under the categories of family, relatives, friends, and so on. Fill in each line and, if necessary, brainstorm examples of additional caring people who offer support, love, and guidance to the child. Then rate each individual according to the degree of support given. Use a scale of 1 to 5 with 5 indicating a high level of support and 1 a very low level of positive involvement.

Family means close and immediate relatives that you live with, and should include your parents and siblings.

Relatives are extended family members such as grandparents, aunts, uncles, and cousins.

Mentors are those special teachers, coaches, or counselors who have helped you learn important lessons.

Role models are people whom you admire and would like to identify with or emulate.

This list can be added to as the child's personal support system increases. Additional activities for processing the important relationships in the child's life are listed at the end of this activity.

MY LOVE AND TRUST SUPPORT NETWORK

Create a network of special people who contribute to your healthy self-esteem and sense of well-being. Then rate each individual according to the degree of support given. Use a scale of 1 to 5 with 5 indicating a high level of support and 1 a very low level of positive involvement.

Immediate Family

Name	Level of Support	Name	Level of Support
_____	_____	_____	_____
_____	_____	_____	_____
_____	_____	_____	_____
_____	_____	_____	_____
_____	_____	_____	_____

Relatives

Name	Level of Support	Name	Level of Support
_____	_____	_____	_____
_____	_____	_____	_____
_____	_____	_____	_____
_____	_____	_____	_____

Friends

Name	Level of Support	Name	Level of Support
_____	_____	_____	_____
_____	_____	_____	_____
_____	_____	_____	_____
_____	_____	_____	_____
_____	_____	_____	_____

Teachers and Mentors

Name	Level of Support	Name	Level of Support
_____	_____	_____	_____
_____	_____	_____	_____
_____	_____	_____	_____
_____	_____	_____	_____
_____	_____	_____	_____

Role Models

Name	Level of Support	Name	Level of Support
_____	_____	_____	_____
_____	_____	_____	_____
_____	_____	_____	_____
_____	_____	_____	_____
_____	_____	_____	_____

ADDITIONAL ACTIVITIES

1. *This is a picture of my family:* (Draw a picture or take a photo of each person in your immediate family involved in an activity. Name each person and describe the activity.)

2. *Relatively speaking:* (Write a story and draw a picture or take a photo of your relatives.)

3. *Important friendships:* (Write a story and draw a picture or take a photo of yourself and one or more of your friends.)

4. *Special teachers or mentors:* (Write a story and draw a picture or take a photo illustrating how a teacher or mentor has helped you.)

5. *Role models in my life:* (Write a story and draw a picture or take a photo describing one of your role models.)

6. *A word about my parents:* (Write a paragraph or story about your parents and draw a picture or take some photos to illustrate the story.)

7. *List some ways your significant others show they care for you:* (Write a paragraph and draw a picture or take some photos to illustrate.)

8. *List some ways you show your significant others how important they are in your life:* (Write a story and draw a picture or take some photos to illustrate.)

Section IV

BLENDED FAMILY

HEALING HURT FEELINGS

GOALS OF THE EXERCISE

1. Identify negative and hurt feelings related to adjusting to a blended family.
2. Develop strategies for coping with painful reactions to family loss and change.
3. Seek solutions that contribute to family harmony.
4. Share cooperative strategies with blended family members.

ADDITIONAL HOMEWORK THAT MAY BE APPLICABLE TO BLENDED FAMILIES

• Abusive Parenting	Measuring Our Feelings	Page 14
• Attention-Deficit/Hyperactivity Disorder (ADHD)	Family Problem Resolution Worksheet	Page 29
• Children with Physical Challenges	Working Together to Create a Plan	Page 102
• Dependent Children/Overprotective Parent	Creating and Cooperating with Family Rules	Page 124

ADDITIONAL PROBLEMS THIS EXERCISE MAY BE MOST USEFUL FOR

• Abusive Parenting
• Divorce
• Dependent Child/Overprotective Parent
• Grief/Loss

SUGGESTIONS FOR USING THIS EXERCISE WITH BLENDED FAMILIES

Negative and hurt feelings are a normal part of adjusting to a blended family. However, when a family member's actions or words create pain, frustration, and confusion, it is important to address the negative emotions by implementing strategies that heal the hurt and that prevent similar problems from occurring in the future. During the adjustment process family members will discover many proactive methods of avoiding discord and promoting family harmony.

The "Healing Hurt Feelings" activity encourages the parents and child to record positive strategies that contribute to the growth of a positive family atmosphere. The ongoing list of healing solutions can be kept in a family journal and referred to whenever a family problem requires an intervention that will result in a positive family outcome. Recognition should be given to each family member who develops and uses a new and successful strategy that contributes to family cohesion and cooperation.

HEALING HURT FEELINGS

Everyone occasionally behaves in a manner that causes problems for others. This is especially true when family members are adjusting to unfamiliar rules, routines, and relationships. Thoughtless or unintentional actions can hurt another person's feelings, damage personal belongings, or interfere with important plans. There are many ways to apologize or to remedy a mistake that has offended or created a hardship for another person. A sincere attempt to heal hurt feelings and reduce the frustration and confusion can reduce overall family friction, and can lead to a loving and harmonious family atmosphere. Read the following suggested list of ways that family members can rebuild damaged or hurt feelings, and brainstorm some additional ideas with your child.

Apologize in person	Include in a game or activity	Rewind your words
Apologize on the phone	Listen to upset feelings	Resist sarcasm and put-downs
Ask, "How can I help?"	Make something	Role play a better way
Agree on a plan	Make up the work	Send flowers
Clean up	Pay for the damage	Share a treat
Do a favor	Practice new procedures	Talk it over
Do extra chores	Replace damaged object	Use an "I" statement
Draw a picture	Rewind your behavior	Use humor
Hold a family meeting	(See the "Rewind Game")	Write a note
Hug frequently		

_____   _____

_____   _____

_____   _____

_____   _____

_____   _____

Work together as a family to record some problematic family interactions on the following lines, and write a remedy or a gesture of restitution that would soothe the hurt feelings or resolve the negative reactions of the injured family member. Use one or a combination of the preceding remedies or create some new solutions that work in your family.

Example: I forgot to take the cookies out of the oven like I promised my stepmom I would. They were burned so badly that we couldn't eat them. She was frustrated and a little angry.

Resolution: I made another batch of cookies and watched them closely, so they turned out perfectly.

Example: I told my stepson that I would watch his soccer game but something important came up at work and I wasn't able to make it until the last few minutes. He was disappointed that I didn't prioritize his game.

Resolution: I apologized to my stepson and asked if I could make it up to him by attending his next two games. He said okay and accepted my apology.

Thoughtless behavior: _____

_____

Resolution: _____

_____

Thoughtless behavior: _____

_____

Resolution: _____

_____

Ask each family member to track their own thoughtless or inadvertent behavior that has negatively created hurt feelings or family discord, write down a potential solution, and implement a plan for restitution. After the problem has been remedied, place a star next to the "Resolution" line to affirm the contribution to family harmony.

Thoughtless behavior: _____

_____

Resolution: _____

_____

Thoughtless behavior: _____

_____

Resolution: _____

_____

Thoughtless behavior: _____

_____

Resolution: _____

_____

Thoughtless behavior: _____

_____

Resolution: _____

_____

Thoughtless behavior: _____

_____

Resolution: _____

_____

Thoughtless behavior: _____

_____

Resolution: _____

_____

Thoughtless behavior: _____

_____

Resolution: _____

_____

Thoughtless behavior: _____

_____

Resolution: _____

_____

UNIQUE ROLES IN OUR BLENDED FAMILY

GOALS OF THE EXERCISE

1. Recognize the unique strengths of each family member.
2. Affirm each individual's positive contributions to the blended family.
3. Encourage positive relationships among blended family members.
4. Create a cooperative and harmonious family environment.

ADDITIONAL HOMEWORK THAT MAY BE
APPLICABLE TO BLENDED FAMILY ISSUES

ADDITIONAL PROBLEMS THIS EXERCISE MAY BE MOST USEFUL FOR

- Divorce
- Grief/Loss
- Poverty-related Issues
- Sibling Rivalry

SUGGESTIONS FOR USING THIS EXERCISE WITH BLENDED FAMILIES

This activity promotes family harmony and positive blended family relationships by structuring the recognition of each family member's unique strengths and contributions to family functioning. Family roles are defined and personal attributes are identified and listed during a family discussion or a scheduled family meeting. The family is encouraged to continue the process of affirming positive characteristics and contributions from individual family members as it evolves into a fully functioning blended family.

UNIQUE ROLES IN OUR BLENDED FAMILY

The process of adjusting to a newly formed blended family takes time, effort, and patience. Each family member possesses unique personality traits and individual strengths and weaknesses. Defining each person's family roles and recognizing individual strengths, assets, and contributions will help to build family unity, harmony, and positive family relationships.

Begin by listing each family member's name and the role they play in the blended family (e.g., Mary Robbins, mom/stepmom, Jared Brown, dad/stepdad, Latecha Brown, sister/stepsister, Jeremy Robbins, brother/stepbrother). Under each name list the personal strengths and contributions attributed to that family member (e.g., compassionate, fun-loving, good cook, humorous, caring, helpful, flexible, energetic, good listener, sensible, athletic, good talker).

Complete this activity together as a family so that the entire blended family recognizes the special talents and importance of each individual. Arrange to update the list frequently as the family evolves and individual family roles, assets, and contributions become more apparent.

Name: _____   Name: _____

Family role: _____   Family role: _____

Assets, strengths, and family contributions: Assets, strengths, and family contributions:

_____   _____

_____   _____

_____   _____

_____   _____

_____   _____

_____   _____

_____   _____

_____   _____

_____   _____

_____   _____

Name: _____

Family role: _____

Assets, strengths, and family contributions:

_____

_____

_____

_____

_____

_____

_____

_____

_____

_____

_____

_____

Name: _____

Family role: _____

Assets, strengths, and family contributions:

_____

_____

_____

_____

_____

_____

_____

_____

_____

_____

_____

_____

Name: _____

Family role: _____

Assets, strengths, and family contributions:

_____

_____

_____

_____

_____

_____

_____

_____

_____

_____

_____

_____

Name: _____

Family role: _____

Assets, strengths, and family contributions:

_____

_____

_____

_____

_____

_____

_____

_____

_____

_____

_____

_____

Name: _____

Family role: _____

Assets, strengths, and family contributions:

_____

_____

_____

_____

_____

_____

_____

_____

_____

_____

_____

_____

Name: _____

Family role: _____

Assets, strengths, and family contributions:

_____

_____

_____

_____

_____

_____

_____

_____

_____

_____

_____

_____

Name: _____

Family role: _____

Assets, strengths, and family contributions:

_____

_____

_____

_____

_____

_____

_____

_____

_____

_____

_____

_____

Name: _____

Family role: _____

Assets, strengths, and family contributions:

_____

_____

_____

_____

_____

_____

_____

_____

_____

_____

_____

_____

BONDING/ATTACHMENT ISSUES

STEPS TO RESPONSIBLE BEHAVIOR

GOALS OF THE EXERCISE

1. Teach the child age-appropriate skills for living.
2. Break chores and tasks down into manageable substeps.
3. Model the chore or task being taught.
4. Affirm the child for learning a new skill.

ADDITIONAL HOMEWORK THAT MAY BE APPLICABLE TO TEACHING RESPONSIBILITY

ADDITIONAL PROBLEMS THIS EXERCISE MAY BE MOST USEFUL FOR

- Gifted/Talented
- Dependent Children/Overprotective Parent
- Strategies for Preschoolers (Ages Birth to 6)
- Strategies for Children (Ages 7 to 12)

SUGGESTIONS FOR USING THIS EXERCISE WITH FAMILIES

This activity prepares the parents to teach the child specific skills necessary for daily functioning, positive interpersonal interaction, and future independence. The process involves choosing a desired skill or behavior and then breaking it down into teachable steps. The parents are directed to model the step-by-step process for the child and to use encouragement and descriptive praise to affirm the child's progress toward the goal. It is recommended that the parents choose only age-appropriate tasks and to limit the lessons to one specific behavior at a time.

STEPS TO RESPONSIBLE BEHAVIOR

Unfortunately, children don't come to us as responsible, self-sufficient entities. It requires parenting and teaching skills to develop the abilities necessary for future independence and successful functioning. The behaviors we hope to see exhibited must be carefully modeled and taught as the child develops and becomes mature enough to perform age-appropriate chores and tasks. Although the time, patience, and energy required to help the child learn to pick up toys, acquire table manners, share possessions, demonstrate social skills, and drive a car safely may seem excessive and frustrating at times, the end result of a well-behaved, responsible, caring, and independent young adult will be well worth the energy.

To teach the child a desired behavior, first identify the specific skill; then break it down into individual steps or subskills. Make certain that the child is mature enough to accomplish the task, and then teach the individual steps required for successful completion.

For example, if the desired chore is to make the bed, the following steps would be required:

1. Smooth out wrinkles in bottom sheet.

2. Pull up top sheet.

3. Pull up covers.

4. Put pillow at the head of the bed.

5. Put on the spread or comforter.

6. Inspect the job for neatness.

7. Congratulate yourself for a job well done.

The process of teaching a child a new skill is most successful when:

*   The skill is a specific rather than a general task (e.g., making the bed is specific, cleaning the bedroom is general).

*   The individual steps or subskills are fully explained and modeled for the child.

*   The chosen skill is age-appropriate.

- The child is given enough time to learn the skill.

- Descriptive praise and encouragement are used to affirm the child for learning a new skill (e.g., You made your bed all by yourself, by pulling up the sheets and covers and putting the pillow neatly at the head).

Prepare to teach your child a desired new behavior or skill by completing the following:

A specific skill I want to teach: _____

The steps involved:

1. _____
2. _____
3. _____
4. _____
5. _____
6. _____
7. _____
8. _____
9. _____
10. _____

Affirmations and encouragement I will give my child while teaching the new skill:

1. _____
2. _____
3. _____
4. _____
5. _____

Each new skill being taught to your child should go through a similar process. It is important not to overwhelm yourself or your child by trying to teach too many skills at once. By focusing upon one skill at a time you will create a positive learning atmosphere, in which both you and your child are rewarded by the positive results of each lesson learned. Keep an ongoing record of the specific skills that have been mastered and refer to them often, as a positive reinforcement for the time and effort given by each of you to teach and learn important life lessons.

A specific skill I want to teach: _____

The steps involved:

1. _____

2. _____

3. _____

4. _____

5. _____

6. _____

7. _____

8. _____

9. _____

10. _____

Affirmations and encouragement I will give my child while teaching the new skill:

1. _____

2. _____

3. _____

4. _____

5. _____

THE BEHAVIOR PROGRESS CHART

GOALS OF THE EXERCISE

1. Encourage the child to engage in positive target behaviors.
2. Define expected behavior in specific terms.
3. Improve the willingness to comply with parents' behavioral requests.
4. Establish the rate of behavioral improvement.
5. Affirm the child for positive behavioral changes.

ADDITIONAL HOMEWORK THAT MAY BE APPLICABLE
TO POSITIVE BEHAVIORAL CHANGES

*   Conduct Disorder/Delinquent   Replacing Noncompliance with   Page 109
    Behavior   Compliance and Cooperation
*   Strategies for Children   Record of Reinforced Behavior   Page 319
    (Ages 7 to 12)   Problem-solving Worksheet   Page 323
*   Strategies for Teenagers   Earning Privileges and Freedoms   Page 335
    (Ages 13 to 18)

ADDITIONAL PROBLEMS THIS EXERCISE MAY BE MOST USEFUL FOR

*   Attention-Deficit/Hyperactivity Disorder (ADHD)
*   Conduct Disorder/Delinquent Behavior
*   Strategies for Children (Ages 7 to 12)
*   Strategies for Teenagers (Ages 13 to 18)

SUGGESTIONS FOR USING THIS EXERCISE WITH PARENTS

This activity teaches parents the importance of framing behavioral expectations in positive rather than negative terms. The parents are asked to name one required behavior and specifically define how the appropriate behavior will look, sound, and feel to them and the child. A baseline of the child's behavior is established, which can be compared with behavioral changes which occur after the parents implement strategies of positive discipline to shape the child's appropriate actions. The parents are directed to utilize affirmations and encouragement to recognize the child's behavioral progress.

THE BEHAVIOR PROGRESS CHART

It is important for both parents and children to picture expected behavior in positive terms rather than trying to eliminate negative behavior through admonishments and punishment. Telling a child what to do or what is expected is more effective than telling a child what not to do, because the first approach plants an image of positive behavior in the child's mind while the second encourages the child to envision negative behavior. Telling a child what is expected instructs the child, while telling a child what not to do gives no information about appropriate alternatives.

To promote positive behavior first list several specific actions that you want to encourage. Be sure to phrase this behavior as a positive action (e.g., please come home by your curfew deadline), rather than in the negative (e.g., don't be late for your curfew). Then describe specifically how this behavior will be recognized (e.g., you will be home on time when you are inside the front door up until 9:00 P.M. on weeknights and 11:00 P.M. on Friday and Saturday nights).

Track the child's current behavior for one week before using any additional disciplinary interventions to modify the behavior. This will give you a baseline to compare any behavior change which results from the interventions you select. After you have established a baseline, describe the expected behavior to the child positively and in detail. When the child complies, affirm the behavior, using low-key descriptive praise and encouraging statements. When the child violates the behavior guideline, implement a positive discipline strategy from the list of suggestions at the bottom of this activity or choose an alternative positive disciplinary strategy. All disciplinary strategies should be delivered with a combination of firmness and kindness. Using anger when disciplining creates a negative atmosphere and actually reduces the effect of the intervention. Failure to follow through with a consequence for behavior violations teaches the child that there is no price to be paid for negative actions.

Choose a behavior you want to help your child develop. You may choose from the list below or create one of you own. Make sure your expected behaviors are stated in the positive.

Complete chores

Sit in chair during meals

Ask for food to be passed

Stay in bed during naps

Stay in bed at night

Pick up toys

Engage in a self-directed activity

Answer the phone appropriately

Play appropriately with siblings

Share toys

Wake up when called

Dress self

Feed pets

Listen when spoken to

Come when called

Say "please" and "thank you"

Shower daily

Comb hair and brush teeth

Complete homework

Replace gas in car

Meet curfew deadline

_____

_____

_____

Use the following steps to create a Behavior Progress Chart for your child.

1. Name the expected target behavior.

    _____

    _____

2. Describe how this behavior will look, sound, and feel to you and your child. (E.g., how will you recognize this behavior?)

    _____

    _____

    _____

    _____

    _____

    _____

3. Track the behavior for up to a week to establish a baseline rate of frequency. Record each occurrence above the day of the week.

    _____   _____   _____   _____   _____   _____   _____
    Mon.   Tues.   Wed.   Thurs.   Fri.   Sat.   Sun.

4. How I plan to promote this behavior with my child. See the following page for suggested interventions to encourage behavioral change.

    _____

    _____

    _____

    _____

    _____

    _____

5. Number of occurrences after the behavior change interventions. Record each occurrence above the day of the week.

    _____   _____   _____   _____   _____   _____   _____
    Mon.   Tues.   Wed.   Thurs.   Fri.   Sat.   Sun.

Suggested Strategies to Promote and Encourage Positive Behavioral Change

1. Name the expected behavior in positive terms and describe specifically how the behavior will be recognized.

2. Use logical consequences to teach the child a more positive way of behaving.

    Example: Broken curfew results in child coming home one hour earlier the next weekday or weekend night.

    Example: Toys not picked up results in loss of toys for a specific period of time.

3. Use contingencies that make all household and family privileges dependent on appropriate behavior.

    Example: Use of family car is contingent upon responsible driving record.

    Example: Playing outside is contingent upon completion of assigned chores.

4. Use choices to define the options the child has.

    Example: "Would it be best to clean your room on Friday or Saturday morning?"

    Example: "Would you rather do your homework before or after dinner?"

5. Give the child a time out or respite from family interaction until the required behavior is evident.

    Example: Child given respite in bedroom until temper tantrum subsides.

    Example: Child given a respite from toys until willing to share with sibling.

6. Use affirmations and encouragement to give low-key recognition of the child's positive behavior.

    Example: "I noticed you finished your homework before dinner."

    Example: "You picked up all of your toys in fifteen minutes."

    Example: "You fed the dog without being asked."

Section VI

CAREER PREPARATION

CAREER FAMILY TREE

GOALS OF THE EXERCISE

1. Increase awareness of the family's history of education and careers.
2. Connect educational experience with career path choices.
3. Identify with the interests, activities, and accomplishments of family members.
4. Consider various educational and occupational opportunities available to the child.

ADDITIONAL HOMEWORK THAT MAY BE APPLICABLE TO CAREER PREPARATION

- Poverty-related Issues   Achieving Family Goals   Page 227

           Different Rules for Home and School   Page 231

- Peer Relationships/Influences   Social Influences in My Child's Life   Page 203
- Gifted/Talented   Teaching Responsibility   Page 162

ADDITIONAL PROBLEMS THIS EXERCISE MAY BE MOST USEFUL FOR

- Gifted/Talented
- Peer Relationships/Influences
- Poverty-related Issues

SUGGESTIONS FOR USING THIS EXERCISE WITH FAMILIES

This activity instructs the parents to enlist their children's help in creating an occupational family history that lists the education and career paths of various nuclear and extended family members. The child is encouraged to interview family members and do research in order to gather information relevant to the education and life's work of current and historical relatives. This family project will help the child focus upon career possibilities and to identify with the interests, activities, and accomplishments of various family members. The "Career Family Tree" is designed to be an ongoing interactive activity that emphasizes the importance of education and work while increasing family historical awareness.

CAREER FAMILY TREE

Exploring the family's history of education, jobs, and occupations can help the child imagine possible careers paths for him- or herself while forming a fuller understanding of the academic or skill training and life work of close and extended family members. Maintaining a career family tree can become a family project that introduces the child to the academic and occupational achievements of family members as far back as family history and memory allow. The project will lead to many family discussions that focus upon the child's relatives' interests and accomplishments. Encourage the child to gather information from other relatives, family records, court documents and/or church records, and by doing a family genealogy search at the library or by using the Internet. Use the following charts to record information about family members, beginning with the mother and father and continuing with extended and blended family members. Review and record new information as it becomes available to keep the project (and the child's interest) dynamic and alive. Be sure to include information about brothers, sisters, aunts and uncles, and the child, as educational and career data becomes relevant.

Name and Relationship:	Education:	Jobs and Occupations:
Example:	High School	Babysitter
Renee Ruiz—Mother	B.A. Teacher Education	Store clerk
	B.A. +20 hours	Library assistant
		Teacher's aide
		Middle school science teacher

Child's Name:

Child's Education:

Child's Jobs and Occupations:

_____ _____ _____

_____ _____ _____

_____ _____

_____ _____

_____ _____

Mother's Name:

_____

_____

Mother's Education:

_____

_____

_____

_____

_____

Mother's Jobs and Occupations:

_____

_____

_____

_____

_____

Father's Name:

_____

_____

Father's Education:

_____

_____

_____

_____

_____

Father's Jobs and Occupations:

_____

_____

_____

_____

Maternal Grandmother's Name:

_____

_____

Maternal Grandmother's Education:

_____

_____

_____

_____

Maternal Grandmother's Jobs and Occupations:

_____

_____

_____

_____

Maternal Grandfather's Name:

_____

_____

Maternal Grandfather's Education:

_____

_____

_____

_____

Maternal Grandfather's Jobs and Occupations:

_____

_____

_____

_____

Paternal Grandmother's Name:

_____

_____

Paternal Grandmother's Education:

_____

_____

_____

_____

Paternal Grandmother's Jobs and Occupations:

_____

_____

_____

_____

Paternal Grandfather's Name:

_____

_____

Paternal Grandfather's Education:

_____

_____

_____

_____

Paternal Grandfather's Jobs and Occupations:

_____

_____

_____

_____

Great-Grandmother's Name:

_____

_____

Great-Grandmother's Education:

_____

_____

_____

_____

Great-Grandmother's Jobs and Occupations:

_____

_____

_____

_____

Great-Grandfather's Name:

_____

_____

Great-Grandfather's Education:

_____

_____

_____

_____

Great-Grandfather's Jobs and Occupations:

_____

_____

_____

_____

Name and Relationship: **Education:**   **Jobs and Occupations:**

_____   _____   _____

_____   _____   _____

      _____   _____

      _____   _____

      _____   _____

_____   _____   _____

_____   _____   _____

      _____   _____

      _____   _____

      _____   _____

      _____   _____

_____   _____   _____

_____   _____   _____

      _____   _____

      _____   _____

      _____   _____

_____   _____   _____

_____   _____   _____

      _____   _____

      _____   _____

      _____   _____

_____   _____   _____

_____   _____   _____

      _____   _____

      _____   _____

SCHOOL-TO-CAREER DIARY

GOALS OF THE EXERCISE

1. Explore career possibilities that interest the child.
2. Identify life experiences that prepare the child for future careers.
3. Outline the educational and skill training requirements of occupations and careers of interest.
4. Use a parent/child collaboration to identify and evaluate various career options.

ADDITIONAL HOMEWORK THAT MAY BE APPLICABLE TO CAREER PREPARATION

• Children with Physical Challenges	Working Together to Create a Plan	Page 102
• School Adjustment Difficulties	My Ideal School Day	Page 252
• Sibling Rivalry	Affirming Each Child's Uniqueness	Page 268
• Strategies for Preschoolers (Ages Birth to 6)	Helping My Child Develop Responsible Behavior	Page 305

ADDITIONAL PROBLEMS THIS EXERCISE MAY BE MOST USEFUL FOR

- Children with Physical Challenges
- School Adjustment Difficulties
- Sibling Rivalry
- Strategies for Preschoolers

SUGGESTIONS FOR USING THIS EXERCISE WITH PARENTS

Career awareness and school-to-work conversations should begin early, as the parents explore various interests and occupational goals with their child. This activity suggests that the child's career-related expectations be used as springboards for discussing future career opportunities and options. The parents are directed to encourage all career-related ideas and expectations rather than discourage or negate unusual or seemingly unrealistic goals as inappropriate or beyond the child's reach. By identifying the early interests and activities and outlining the educational requirements relevant to future careers, the parents can help the child determine career choices that match up with the child's aptitude, ability, and dreams. Many worthwhile career options are discovered along the path to the child's early career dreams.

SCHOOL-TO-CAREER DIARY

INSTRUCTIONS FOR THE PARENTS

From a very early age children are interested in the careers and occupations they learn about from family members, friends, community activities, books, TV, and other media sources. Children dream about becoming everything from a truck driver to president, nurse to C.E.O. of a large corporation. When children's dreams appear unrealistic (e.g., rock star or astronaut), parents and teachers often try to discourage the goal or redirect the child's thinking. Perhaps a better way to react to what seems to be a farfetched career choice is to help the child understand the steps necessary to achieve the goal. A child may wish to become a professional football player but not understand the years of dedication, practice, physical demands, and academic requirements indicated. Another child may dream of becoming a movie star without considering the necessary academic training, dramatic coaching, and years of dedication and persistence endured by most successful actors. This activity will assist the child in analyzing career choices more realistically without discouraging any dreams for future excellence. Career ideas will evolve and become more individually appropriate as the child matures. A child who originally wanted to be a ballerina may decide to become a physical education or yoga teacher; however, the basic dream was not decimated—it simply became more appropriate. In the process of pursuing a career dream a child learns many important life lessons. The parent's job is to acknowledge the dream, while providing useful and practical information the child can use before the final career choice is made.

Brainstorm as many jobs, occupations, and career choices that might be of interest to the child in the future. Be as creative as possible and try not to limit the child or yourself by listing only realistic or possible ideas. Consider this an ongoing list that will grow and evolve as the child matures and becomes more aware of his or her career possibilities.

_____   _____   _____

_____   _____   _____

_____   _____   _____

_____   _____   _____

_____   _____   _____

_____   _____   _____

_____   _____   _____

_____   _____   _____

_____   _____   _____

_____   _____   _____

_____   _____   _____

_____   _____   _____

_____   _____   _____

Now ask the child to select several favorite occupations to consider in more detail. List the child's choices, and indicate the child's age at the time of the selection. Indicate the various tasks typically performed in this profession and list the various ways the child can begin to prepare for that career. Finally list the educational and skill training requirements of the profession. As the child matures, more research can be done into possible career choices with the help of library resources, the Internet, and information available from the school counselor.

Repeat this activity frequently as the child's ideas about future careers grow and change. This diary can be kept as a record of the child's career interests as they evolve from an early age. The parent/child discussions generated, and information gathered, will help the child realize the numerous career possibilities that are available, and will assist him or her in making a well-informed decision about an extremely important issue.

Example:

Child's Name and Age: Jimmy, age 7

Profession of Interest: Carpenter

Type of Work Involved: Build things, construct houses and buildings, remodel buildings, create new concepts for more efficient living.

Life Experiences That Prepare for the Future Career: Playing with blocks, building toys, constructing models, observing construction projects, elementary mathematics, elementary art classes, building projects with parents and friends, trips to hardware store with parent, watching home improvement shows on TV, projects created in extracurricular activity groups, Junior Achievement, community volunteer projects.

Educational and Skill Training Recommendations and/or Requirements: Building projects at home and at school, skill training classes offered in secondary school, postsecondary trade/technical school, community college, apprenticeship, job shadow experience, internships in building and construction.

Child's name and age: _____

Profession of interest: _____

Type of work involved: _____

_____

_____

_____

_____

Life experiences that prepare for the future career: _____

_____

_____

_____

_____

Educational and skill training recommendations and/or requirements: _____

_____

_____

_____

_____

Child's name and age: _____

Profession of interest: _____

Type of work involved: _____

_____

_____

_____

Life experiences that prepare for the future career: _____

_____

_____

_____

Educational and skill training recommendations and/or requirements: _____

_____

_____

_____

_____

Child's name and age: _____

Profession of interest: _____

Type of work involved: _____

_____

_____

_____

Life experiences that prepare for the future career: _____

_____

_____

_____

Educational and skill training recommendations and/or requirements: _____

_____

_____

_____

_____

Section VII

CHARACTER DEVELOPMENT

DIVISION OF FAMILY LABOR

GOALS OF THE EXERCISE

1. Identify essential responsibilities that support family functioning.
2. Distribute chores and tasks among family members.
3. Recognize the contributions of individual family members.
4. Encourage all family members to contribute to the well-being of the family.

ADDITIONAL HOMEWORK THAT MAY BE APPLICABLE TO FAMILY COHESION

• Gifted/Talented	Teaching Responsibility	Page 162
• Poverty-related Issues	Achieving Family Goals	Page 227
• Sibling Rivalry	Affirming Each Child's Uniqueness	Page 268
• Strategies for Teenagers (Ages 13 to 18)	Earning Privileges and Freedoms	Page 335

ADDITIONAL PROBLEMS THIS EXERCISE MAY BE MOST USEFUL FOR

- Attention-Deficit/Hyperactivity Disorder (ADHD)
- Attention-seeking Behavior
- Dependent Child/Overprotective Parent
- Oppositional Defiant Behavior

SUGGESTIONS FOR USING THIS EXERCISE WITH FAMILIES

Parents can increase the child's awareness of the jobs and responsibilities necessary for the basic family functioning by brainstorming and recording all jobs essential for family well-being. Many responsibilities already assumed by the parents can be assigned to the children, based on their age and level of maturity. By assuming part of the family workload, children can develop responsibility, build self-esteem, and acquire positive character traits, which come from personal contribution and effort. The parents are directed to assign family jobs on a weekly basis during a family meeting, and to recognize individual family members for jobs well done the previous week.

DIVISION OF FAMILY LABOR

Work together as a family to develop a list of all the tasks, chores, and duties that are necessary for the family to function smoothly and effectively. Include both large and small jobs that are performed by each family member, including parents and children. Select from the suggestions below and add new ideas to create an inventory that represents the specific needs and requirements of your family.

After brainstorming a complete family labor inventory, determine who will perform each duty by holding a job auction to assign each job to a family member, making sure that the assignment is age-appropriate and within that person's ability level. The parents will probably assume the income-earning duties and other larger responsibilities, while the children can help with the smaller jobs. The children's participation in the family labor will increase as they grow older and more mature. Make sure that each person is recognized for the contributions they make to the family operation and organization. Giving back to the family by completing important and necessary jobs helps a child feel responsible and needed. The efforts contributed eventually become labors of love, and are a major building block to character development and healthy self-esteem.

This activity will help all family members realize how important each job is, and how much each family member is contributing. Children become aware of the many responsibilities assumed by their parents that they may have previously taken for granted. By equitably dividing the family jobs, both parents and children can play an essential role in supporting the family and participating in building the loving bonds that promote family cohesion and unity.

Answer phone

Assist grandparents

Assist sick family member

Attend family outings

Attend school activities

Attend school conferences

Baby-sit

Clean house

Clean kitchen counter

Clean room

Clean sink, tub, and toilet

Clear table

Collect dirty clothes

Cook dinner

Decorate the house

Do homework

Do laundry

Dust

Earn income

Feed pet(s)

Fold laundry

Garden

Get dressed

Get ready for bed

Get ready for school

Grocery shop

Hang up coat

Homework helper

Iron clothes

Load dishwasher

Maintain car

Make breakfast

Make lunch

Mend clothing

Mop floor

Mow lawn

Pay bills

Pick up bathroom

Pick up toys or belongings

Plan social events

Prepare family budget

Repair roof

Run errands

Set table

Shop for clothes

Shovel walks

Start dinner

Take child to doctor

Take out the trash

Vacuum

Wash car

Wash windows

_____

_____

_____

_____

_____

_____

_____

_____

_____

_____

Family Job Assignments

Meet once a week with all family members to identify and assign the jobs and responsibilities necessary for the basic operations of the family. Some assignments will remain the same, while others may be moved from one family member to another. Make sure that each family member is given an essential responsibility, and thank each person for the important work that was completed the previous week.

Example:

Date: Mon., Sept. 9   Job: Oil change for car   Person responsible: Dad

Date: _____   Job: _____   Person responsible: _____

Date: _____   Job: _____   Person responsible: _____

Date: _____   Job: _____   Person responsible: _____

Date: _____   Job: _____   Person responsible: _____

Date: _____   Job: _____   Person responsible: _____

Date: _____   Job: _____   Person responsible: _____

Date: _____   Job: _____   Person responsible: _____

Date: _____   Job: _____   Person responsible: _____

Date: _____   Job: _____   Person responsible: _____

Date: _____   Job: _____   Person responsible: _____

Date: _____   Job: _____   Person responsible: _____

Date: _____   Job: _____   Person responsible: _____

Date: _____   Job: _____   Person responsible: _____

Date: _____   Job: _____   Person responsible: _____

Date: _____   Job: _____   Person responsible: _____

Date: _____   Job: _____   Person responsible: _____

Date: _____   Job: _____   Person responsible: _____

Date: _____   Job: _____   Person responsible: _____

Date: _____   Job: _____   Person responsible: _____

Date: _____   Job: _____   Person responsible: _____

Date: _____   Job: _____   Person responsible: _____

Date: _____   Job: _____   Person responsible: _____

Date: _____   Job: _____   Person responsible: _____

Date: _____   Job: _____   Person responsible: _____

SHARING THE FAMILY RESOURCES

GOALS OF THE EXERCISE

1. List the various resources provided by the family.
2. Recognize the fulfilled needs and contributions of each family member.
3. Identify the unmet needs of family members.
4. Identify additional contributions that can be made to sustain the family resource bank.

ADDITIONAL HOMEWORK THAT MAY BE APPLICABLE TO CHARACTER DEVELOPMENT

• Attention-seeking Behavior	Family Job Support Checklist	Page 37
• Blended Family	Healing Hurt Feelings	Page 49
	Unique Roles in Our Blended Family	Page 53
• Divorce/Separation	Assuming Our Parental Responsibilities	Page 145

ADDITIONAL PROBLEMS THIS EXERCISE MAY BE MOST USEFUL FOR

- Attention-seeking Behavior
- Blended Family
- Divorce

SUGGESTIONS FOR USING THIS EXERCISE WITH FAMILIES

Children often view the process of getting their needs met as a one-way street, where they demand, and another family member either does or does not provide. This perception views the family resources as finite and only able to accommodate a limited number of needs. One essential aspect of character development is to define the family resources in terms of the needs and contributions of each of its members. The family resources become much greater when each family member shares in the overall task of providing for the group as a whole. This concept of giving and getting helps each family member assume a cooperative rather than a competitive attitude toward participation in the family unit.

SHARING THE FAMILY RESOURCES

Each family member has basic needs which are ideally provided by sharing the family resources. Basic needs include food, shelter, love, relationships, and learning how to survive. Many families also provide additional support (e.g., financial assistance, transportation, food preparation, skill development, religious education, character development, and so on). Following is a list of ways that families accommodate their members. Read the list and brainstorm some additional ideas during a family meeting. Remember that all families provide for some of these needs but no families provide them all.

Active listening	Extended friendships	Problem solving
Advice	Family get-togethers	Protection
Allowance	Family history	Responsibility training
Attention	Financial support	School supplies
Birthday celebrations	Food	Skill development
Character training	Food preparation	Sports equipment
Child care	Games	Time
Church affiliation	Gardening	Toys
Clothing	Homework support	Transportation
Community associations	Housecleaning help	Unconditional positive regard
Educational support	Hugs	
Entertainment	Love	Vacations
Empathy	Mentoring	Volunteer work
Etiquette	Pride	Yard work

Brainstorm some additional ideas at a family meeting:

_____   _____   _____

_____   _____   _____

_____   _____   _____

_____   _____   _____

Now assign each family member to list the family resources they use and the contributions they return to the family resource bank. Have each person consider areas where their needs are not being fully met and areas where they could make a larger contribution to support other family members. Families function best when each member contributes to make sure that the needs of all are met.

Example:

Name or Role: Mother

Resources Used:	**Resources Contributed:**
Love	Financial support
Problem solving	Food preparation
Entertainment	Time
Hugs	Child care
Pride	Educational support
Unmet Needs:	**Additional Contributions I Could Make:**
Active listening	Skill development
Empathy	Responsibility training
Housecleaning help	Family history

Name or Role: _____

Resources Used:	**Resources Contributed:**
_____	_____
_____	_____
_____	_____
_____	_____
_____	_____
Unmet Needs:	**Additional Contributions I Could Make:**
_____	_____
_____	_____
_____	_____
_____	_____

Name or Role: _____

Resources Used: **Resources Contributed:**

_____   _____

_____   _____

_____   _____

_____   _____

_____   _____

Unmet Needs: **Additional Contributions I Could Make:**

_____   _____

_____   _____

_____   _____

_____   _____

_____   _____

Name or Role: _____

Resources Used: **Resources Contributed:**

_____   _____

_____   _____

_____   _____

_____   _____

_____   _____

Unmet Needs: **Additional Contributions I Could Make:**

_____   _____

_____   _____

_____   _____

_____   _____

Name or Role: _____

Resources Used: **Resources Contributed:**

_____   _____

_____   _____

_____   _____

_____   _____

_____   _____

_____   _____

Unmet Needs: **Additional Contributions I Could Make:**

_____   _____

_____   _____

_____   _____

_____   _____

_____   _____

_____   _____

Name or Role: _____

Resources Used: **Resources Contributed:**

_____   _____

_____   _____

_____   _____

_____   _____

_____   _____

Unmet Needs: **Additional Contributions I Could Make:**

_____   _____

_____   _____

_____   _____

_____   _____

_____   _____

Section VIII

CHILDREN WITH PHYSICAL CHALLENGES

STRATEGIES FOR SUPPORTING OUR CHILD WITH PHYSICAL CHALLENGES

GOALS OF THE EXERCISE

1. Identify specific concerns of the parents and the special needs child.
2. Use a solution-oriented approach to reduce anxiety.
3. Maintain a record of ongoing problems and attempted strategies for resolution.
4. Reduce feelings of helplessness and/or hopelessness.

ADDITIONAL HOMEWORK THAT MAY BE APPLICABLE TO FAMILIES DEALING WITH PHYSICAL CHALLENGES

- Grief/Loss   Grief and Loss Circle of Support   Page 188
- Peer Relationships/Influences   Peer Pressures, Values, and Influences   Page 207
- Posttraumatic Stress Disorder   Reframing Our Worries   Page 216
  (PTSD)
- Strategies for Teenagers   Listening with Empathy   Page 330
  Ages (13 to 18)

ADDITIONAL PROBLEMS THIS EXERCISE MAY BE MOST USEFUL FOR

- Depression
- Divorce
- Grief/Loss
- Peer Relationships/Influences
- Posttraumatic Stress Disorder (PTSD)

SUGGESTIONS FOR USING THIS EXERCISE WITH FAMILIES

Parents and children with physical challenges often experience excessive generalized anxiety caused by undefined worries and concerns that remain unaddressed and unresolved. This activity directs the parents to name their concerns and then use a solution-oriented approach to define a positive outcome and to identify possible strategies that will contribute to that outcome. The parents are guided to begin with an immediate problem and then move to longer-term issues of concern. The problem-solving worksheets can be maintained as an ongoing record of solutions generated by the parents and child working together to overcome challenges.

INSTRUCTIONS FOR THE PARENTS

Brainstorm a list of all the concerns and challenges you may encounter as your child with physical challenges matures. Include medical, physical, social, academic, emotional, and behavioral issues. The list will evolve over time, as new problems arise and old concerns are overcome. This activity can be used as an ongoing diary to record the child's and the family's progress in solving the many unique difficulties faced by children with special needs. Using a problem-solving approach will give the child, parents, and siblings a sense of hope and accomplishment as success is achieved in overcoming both large and small challenges.

Review the following list and create a personalized list of concerns specific to the child with physical challenges and to your unique family situation. Then develop a list of potential solutions and strategies that will be effective in meeting and overcoming those concerns. Begin the process by developing strategies to address immediate concerns (e.g., evaluation of the condition, medical intervention, preschool accommodations) and then move to larger and longer-term issues (e.g., independent living skills, college and career preparation).

Concerns:

Accommodations at church	Family stress	Recreational activities
Accommodations at school	Independent functioning	Respite for parents
Child care	Medical treatment	Self-esteem of child
Developing social skills	Mental stimulation	Sibling interaction
Discipline strategies	Peer group interaction	
Educating friends and family	Physical exercise	

Personalize the List for Your Child and Family:

_____   _____   _____

_____   _____   _____

_____   _____   _____

_____   _____   _____

_____   _____   _____

_____   _____   _____

_____   _____   _____

_____   _____   _____

_____   _____   _____

Choose an immediate challenge and plan some strategies to address that concern.

Example:

Concern or Worry:

Our child with Asperger's Disorder is afraid or unwilling to try new things. He becomes resistant and often cries or throws a mini temper tantrum when confronted with an unfamiliar situation.

Positive Outcome:

Our child participates in new experiences and verbalizes anxiety-producing thoughts.

Potential Strategies:

- Inform child of the new activity in advance.

- List the sequential steps involved in the activity.

- Create a pleasant or positive last step in the activity as a reward for participation.

- Actively listen to and address the child's anxieties.

- Debrief the activity with the child, using conversation, pictures, and photos.

STRATEGIES FOR SUPPORTING OUR CHILD WITH PHYSICAL CHALLENGES

Identify a worry or concern and define a positive outcome for the problem. Then list several strategies that will help you and your child overcome that challenge.

Worry or Concern	Positive Outcome	Potential Strategies

WORKING TOGETHER TO CREATE A PLAN

GOALS OF THE EXERCISE

1. Establish short-, mid-, and long-term goals with the child.
2. Break goals down into manageable and sequential steps.
3. Identify the need to involve outside resources to achieve the goals.
4. Develop an optimistic attitude toward future goal achievement.

ADDITIONAL HOMEWORK THAT MAY BE APPLICABLE TO FAMILIES DEALING WITH PHYSICAL CHALLENGES

• Depression	Creating Positive Self-Talk	Page 130
• Divorce/Separation	Assuming Our Parental Responsibilities	Page 145
• Gifted/Talented	Procedures for Meals, Bedtime, and the Morning Routine	Page 165
• Eating Disorder	Beautiful on the Inside	Page 152

ADDITIONAL PROBLEMS THIS EXERCISE MAY BE MOST USEFUL FOR

- Depression
- Divorce
- Grief/Loss
- Gifted/Talented
- Eating Disorder

SUGGESTIONS FOR USING THIS EXERCISE WITH FAMILIES

This activity directs parents and the child with physical disabilities to identify short-, mid-, and long-term goals that will establish a realistic and positive quality of life for the child. The goals are then broken down into manageable steps to increase the probability of goal achievement. The parents are asked to determine which of the short-term objectives can be accomplished internally and which will require outside resources to support the efforts of the child and family. Each step toward goal achievement is recognized as a method of increasing resolve and contributing to a "can do" attitude in the child and family.

WORKING TOGETHER TO CREATE A PLAN

INSTRUCTIONS FOR THE PARENTS

Creating a plan of action to achieve both long- and short-term goals can focus the child with physical challenges and the family on positive outcomes rather than dwelling on the obstacles to goal achievement. A positive approach to goal attainment can empower both the parents and the child to apply their own strengths and resources toward obtaining a positive and realistic quality of life and to seek outside resources if necessary. Both long- and short-term goals should be realistic and attainable, based on an objective assessment of the child's and the family's strengths and resources. However, creative thinking and high expectations can often lead to outcomes that at first appear to be out of reach.

Begin by listing several short-, mid-, and long-term goals that the family and child agree are important. Examples follow; however, your list should reflect the individual needs and desires of the child and the family.

Examples:

Short-term Goals:	Mid-term Goals:	Long-term Goals:
Dress self	Attend school	Finish high school
Feed self	Learn to walk	Attend college
Exercise regularly	Increase upper body strength	Live independently
Verbalize needs	Complete homework	Attain employment

Create a Personalized List of Goals for Your Child:

Short-term Goals:	Mid-term Goals:	Long-term Goals:
_____	_____	_____
_____	_____	_____
_____	_____	_____
_____	_____	_____
_____	_____	_____

Pick one goal to focus on: _____

Goals must be broken down into individual steps or short-term objectives for their attainment. Even short-term goals such as dressing oneself involve smaller steps that must be learned and accomplished one at a time (e.g., pulling on socks, buttoning shirt, pulling up pants). The identification of these smaller steps will keep the child on track to achieve the ultimate goal. Try to list the short-term objectives sequentially so that they can be checked off and celebrated when accomplished. Each time the child obtains mastery over a short-term objective it strengthens resolve and increases the probability that the ultimate goal will be achieved.

First, identify the short-term objectives leading to goal attainment:

_____   _____

_____   _____

_____   _____

_____   _____

Next, determine which steps the child and family can take toward goal attainment and which steps will require assistance from an outside resource (e.g., physical therapist, teacher, counselor, physician).

Steps we can take: Necessary outside resources:

_____   _____

_____   _____

_____   _____

_____   _____

_____   _____

This plan was developed in a cooperative effort by:

_____ _____ _____

_____ _____ _____

_____ _____ _____

_____ _____ _____

Date: _____

CONDUCT DISORDER/ DELINQUENT BEHAVIOR

REPLACING NONCOMPLIANCE WITH COMPLIANCE AND COOPERATION

GOALS OF THE EXERCISE

1. Identify negative behavior patterns that are problematic for the child and the family.
2. Name the negative behavior, using short, specific behavioral terms.
3. Teach the child positive alternatives to negative behavior.
4. Affirm the child for positive behavioral changes.

ADDITIONAL HOMEWORK THAT MAY BE APPLICABLE TO FAMILIES DEALING WITH CONDUCT DISORDER

• Attention-Deficit/Hyperactivity Disorder (ADHD)	Family Problem Resolution Worksheet	Page 23
• Oppositional Defiant Disorder (ODD)	Planning for Disruptive Behavior	Page 194
• Strategies for Preschoolers (Ages Birth to 6)	Helping My Child Develop Responsible Behavior	Page 305
• Strategies for Children (Ages 7 to 12)	Record of Reinforced Behavior	Page 319

ADDITIONAL PROBLEMS THIS EXERCISE MAY BE MOST USEFUL FOR

- Attention-Deficit/Hyperactivity Disorder (ADHD)
- Oppositional Defiant Disorder (ODD)
- Strategies for Preschoolers (Ages Birth to 6)
- Strategies for Children (Ages 7 to 12)
- Strategies for Teenagers (Ages 13 to 18)

SUGGESTIONS FOR USING THIS EXERCISE WITH FAMILIES

This activity teaches parents to modify their child's unacceptable behavior by helping the child replace a negative action with a positive action. The parents are guided to use three steps to extinguish negative behavior: (1) Identify and name the negative behavior;

(2) Clearly indicate that the behavior is unacceptable; (3) Describe, model, and teach the child a new appropriate behavior. Initially the parents create a sequential list of their child's unacceptable behavior and then brainstorm acceptable behavioral alternatives with the child. The parents and child choose three behaviors to modify and then follow the steps to create a positive behavioral change.

REPLACING NONCOMPLIANCE WITH COMPLIANCE AND COOPERATION

INSTRUCTIONS FOR THE PARENTS

Negative, inappropriate behavior needs to be replaced with positive, appropriate actions if the child is to learn new methods of coping with daily problems and challenges. It doesn't work well to tell the child what not to do without describing and modeling an alternative and more acceptable behavior. It is far more effective to tell the child what to do and by indicating what behavior is approved and is consistent with the family rules.

Telling a child not to eat dessert before dinner simply calls the child's attention to the very behavior we are hoping to discourage, while telling the child that dessert may be eaten after dinner plants an image of appropriate behavior in the child's mind. Three effective steps toward eliminating a negative behavior are:

- Name the inappropriate behavior.

- Clearly indicate that the behavior is unacceptable.

- Describe, model, and teach a new, appropriate behavior.

Begin by specifically identifying all the negative behaviors that you would like to see eliminated from your child's repertoire. Give each behavior a short, specific name that you can use when addressing the behavior with your child (e.g., swearing, biting, kicking, taunting, curfew violation, neglected chores, stealing, or threatening). Next, prioritize the behaviors sequentially in the order of their disturbing nature and the disruption they cause to the child and the family. Then brainstorm with your child a list of alternative positive behaviors that can be substituted for each negative action. Some examples follow:

Problematic Behavior Listed in Order of Severity: **Positive Actions to Acquire:**

_____   _____

_____   _____

_____   _____

_____   _____

Negative Actions to Eliminate:	Positive Actions to Acquire:
Swearing	Use approved vocabulary only
Curfew violation	Come home on time
Neglected chores	Complete chores by deadline
Property destruction	Respect other's property
Aggressive behavior	Verbally express frustration
Threatening actions	Use conflict resolution skills

Choose one problematic behavior and follow the steps to extinguish the behavior.

Example:

1. Name the behavior: *Swearing*

2. Describe why the behavior is unacceptable: *Swearing is vulgar and socially unacceptable. It is against our family rules and the rules at school and church.*

3. Describe the acceptable, alternative behavior: *Develop a vocabulary of feeling words and phrases that expresses anger and frustration without vulgarity.*

1. Name the behavior: _____.

2. Describe why the behavior is unacceptable: _____
   _____

3. Describe the acceptable, alternative behavior: _____
   _____

Select six more problems to extinguish and complete the steps alone or with your child.

1. Name the behavior: _____

2. Describe why the behavior is unacceptable: _____
   _____

3. Describe the acceptable, alternative behavior: _____
   _____

1. Name the behavior: _____.

2. Describe why the behavior is unacceptable: _____
   _____

3. Describe the acceptable, alternative behavior: _____
   _____

1. Name the behavior: _____

2. Describe why the behavior is unacceptable: _____
    _____

3. Describe the acceptable, alternative behavior: _____
    _____

1. Name the behavior: _____

2. Describe why the behavior is unacceptable: _____
    _____

3. Describe the acceptable, alternative behavior: _____
    _____

1. Name the behavior: _____

2. Describe why the behavior is unacceptable: _____
    _____

3. Describe the acceptable, alternative behavior: _____
    _____

1. Name the behavior: _____

2. Describe why the behavior is unacceptable: _____
    _____

3. Describe the acceptable, alternative behavior: _____
    _____

Remember to encourage the child whenever appropriate behavior is noted, and affirm how much the behavior is appreciated and how it contributes to the overall family harmony.

USING PRIVILEGES AS CONTINGENCIES AND CONSEQUENCES

GOALS OF THE EXERCISE

1. Differentiate between entitlements and privileges.
2. Recognize the many privileges granted by the family.
3. Make privileges contingent on the child's positive behavior.
4. Use privileges as consequences to extinguish the child's negative behavior.

ADDITIONAL HOMEWORK THAT MAY BE APPLICABLE TO FAMILIES DEALING WITH CONDUCT DISORDER

- Attention Deficit/Hyperactivity Disorder (ADHD)
  - Family Problem Resolution Worksheet — Page 29
- Oppositional Defiant Disorder (ODD)
  - Planning for Disruptive Behavior — Page 194
- Strategies for Preschoolers (Ages Birth to 6)
  - Helping My Child Develop Responsible Behavior — Page 305
- Strategies for Children (Ages 7 to 12)
  - Record of Reinforced Behavior — Page 319

ADDITIONAL PROBLEMS THIS EXERCISE MAY BE MOST USEFUL FOR

- Attention-Deficit/Hyperactivity Disorder (ADHD)
- Children with Physical Challenges
- Eating Disorder
- Strategies for Preschoolers (Ages Birth to 6)

SUGGESTIONS FOR USING THIS EXERCISE WITH FAMILIES

This activity helps parents to differentiate between privileges that can be granted when the child's behavior is compliant and cooperative and withdrawn when negative behavior becomes a problem. The parents are directed to brainstorm a list of family privileges with their child and to indicate that the list will be used as potential consequences to encourage the child to engage in behavior that contributes to the harmonious functioning of the family. When negative behavior does occur, the child is asked to select an appropriate loss of privilege as a consequence, to encourage future appropriate behavior. If the child fails to make an effective choice, the parent makes the decision. An ongoing record of the process is kept to evaluate the effectiveness of privileges used as contingencies to create positive behavior change.

USING PRIVILEGES AS CONTINGENCIES AND CONSEQUENCES

INSTRUCTIONS FOR THE PARENTS

Privileges can be used as contingencies or consequences to shape a child's cooperation, compliance, and positive behavior. Too often both parents and children confuse privileges, which should be granted to the child based upon acceptable behavior, with entitlements, which are due to the child regardless of the level of cooperation. When privileges are used as contingencies, only the basic needs are granted as entitlements. Everything else is a privilege that must be earned through the child's contributions and cooperation.

Using this approach promotes responsible behavior and a cooperative attitude in the child. Children develop healthy self-esteem when they realize that they have significant control in determining their own quality of life based upon the contributions they make to the overall family functioning. They soon learn that cooperation brings them positive results and resistance and/or negative behavior causes negative consequences.

Using the theory that most family assets are privileges that must be earned, brainstorm with the child a list of family resources that can be distributed based on positive and cooperative performance. Remember that both small and large favors can be utilized as a consequence to reward positive behavior or to modify negative behavior.

Examples of Privileges That can be Used as Contingencies:

Playing with toys	Snacks
Listening to music	Riding bike to store
Playing outside	Rides to school
Computer time	Staying up later
Playing inside	New clothes
Watching TV	Playing a game with parent
Helping with homework	Playing video games

Brainstorm with your child to create an extensive list of family privileges:

_____	_____
_____	_____
_____	_____
_____	_____
_____	_____
_____	_____
_____	_____
_____	_____
_____	_____
_____	_____
_____	_____
_____	_____
_____	_____
_____	_____

Use the list you have created when the child's behavior becomes problematic and/or disruptive to the family harmony. Indicate to the child that the negative behavior will result in the loss of a privilege. Give the child an opportunity to select an appropriate privilege to be used as a consequence. Explain that the loss of the privilege is designed to encourage more appropriate behavior in the future; therefore, the privilege selected should be somehow related to the problem and significant enough for positive learning to occur. Make it clear that if the child refuses or is unable to choose an appropriate loss of a privilege, the parent will make the choice. This approach makes the process successful with both cooperative and manipulative children.

Keep an ongoing record of problem situations, privileges lost, and subsequent behavior changes in the space following. This will identify how the process is working with your child and indicate which privileges are most successful in encouraging positive behavior. Note any changes recommended by you or the child to make the process more effective in the future.

Inappropriate behavior:

_____

_____

_____

_____

Privilege selected by the child as a reasonable consequence:

_____

Parent approves the child's choice as a reasonable consequence:

Yes _____ No _____

Reason(s) for approval or disapproval:

_____

_____

_____

_____

Alternative privilege selected by the parent to teach future appropriate behavior:

_____

_____

_____

_____

Behavior changes resulting from the loss of the privilege:

_____

_____

_____

_____

Recommended changes for the next time the inappropriate behavior occurs:

_____

_____

_____

DEPENDENT CHILDREN/
OVERPROTECTIVE PARENT

OVERPROTECTIVE PARENT VERSUS POSITIVE PARENT

GOALS OF THE EXERCISE

1. Identify inappropriate or excessive worries regarding the child's welfare.
2. Translate excessive worries into realistic parent expectations.
3. Reduce the parent's level of stress.
4. Develop independence, responsibility, and healthy self-esteem in the child.

ADDITIONAL HOMEWORK THAT MAY BE APPLICABLE TO FAMILIES WITH DEPENDENT CHILDREN

ADDITIONAL PROBLEMS THIS EXERCISE MAY BE MOST USEFUL FOR

- Attention-Deficit/Hyperactivity Disorder (ADHD)
- Children with Physical Challenges
- Eating Disorder
- Strategies for Preschoolers (Ages Birth to 6)

SUGGESTIONS FOR USING THIS EXERCISE WITH FAMILIES

Excessive worry and overinvolvement can interfere with the parent-child relationship and with the ability to parent effectively. The child may become overly dependent and resentful of the parent's lack of confidence and trust. This activity directs the parent to review excessive worries and overprotective tendencies with their co-parent and/or counselor and to reframe them into proactive and positive parent expectations. One worry is selected for immediate focus and proactive strategies are developed. The parent is asked to note changes observed in the child's behavior and in their own level of stress and parenting effectiveness resulting from their more effective approach.

OVERPROTECTIVE PARENT VERSUS POSITIVE PARENT

INSTRUCTIONS FOR THE PARENTS

Excessive worry and overprotective tendencies can actually interfere with the parent-child relationship and with the ability to parent effectively. Many parents are anxious and extremely cautious with their first newborn; however, the degree of worry and the level of stress usually decline to a normal level as the child matures and the parents become more confident. However, in some cases the tendency to over-parent continues beyond the normal adjustment period. This can create an overly dependent child and interfere with the development of responsibility, independence, and healthy self-esteem.

Review your child-related worries and consider whether they are realistic or excessive. Discuss your worry list with your co-parent and/or counselor to gain an independent perspective. List your persistent worries in the space provided. Then try to reframe each worry into a positive expectation for yourself and your child. Examples of overprotective fears and worries versus positive/proactive parent expectations follow.

Overprotective Fears and Worries	Positive/proactive Parent Expectations
Child may get sick	Provide routine health checkups
Child isn't eating nutritiously	Provide healthy food choices
Not enough friends	Provide play opportunities and teach friendship skills
May get hurt	Child can survive routine bumps and bruises
Drives too fast	Using car contingent on responsible driving
Low grades	Plan with child to address achievement issues

Create a list of your current child-related worries and translate them into realistic and proactive expectations.

Overprotective Fears and Worries	**Positive/proactive Parent Expectations**

Choose a worry that you would like to reframe into a positive parent expectation. Describe how this more realistic approach will reduce your level of stress and will assist the child to become more independent and responsible. Record any changes you observe in yourself and your child resulting from your more proactive strategies.

A worry that interferes with my positive parenting is:

_____

_____

I will reframe this worry as follows:

_____

_____

This will change my parenting and will encourage my child to become more responsible and self-sufficient by:

_____

_____

_____

_____

_____

I observe the following changes as a result of my positive/proactive parent expectations:

_____

_____

_____

_____

_____

_____

CREATING AND COOPERATING WITH FAMILY RULES

GOALS OF THE EXERCISE

1. Establish family rules for appropriate behavior.
2. Consolidate family rules into guidelines that are positive and broad.
3. Encourage all family members to demonstrate respectful, responsible, and loving behavior.
4. Determine how consequences will be developed.

ADDITIONAL HOMEWORK THAT MAY BE APPLICABLE
TO FAMILIES WITH DEPENDENT CHILDREN

• Bonding/Attachment Issues	Steps to Responsible Behavior	Page 60
• Character Development	Division of Family Labor	Page 86
	Sharing the Family Resources	Page 90
• Conduct Disorder/ Delinquent Behavior	Using Privileges as Contingencies and Consequences	Page 114
• Gifted/Talented	Procedures for Meals, Bedtime, and the Morning Routine	Page 165

ADDITIONAL PROBLEMS THIS EXERCISE MAY BE MOST USEFUL FOR

- Blended Family
- Character Development
- Conduct Disorder
- Gifted/Talented

SUGGESTIONS FOR USING THIS EXERCISE WITH FAMILIES

Using a cooperative effort to establish rules and broad positive guidelines will enlist each family member's support in promoting a safe, effective, and loving family atmosphere. The family is directed to brainstorm all rules necessary for effective family functioning and then to categorize them into broader guidelines that will shape behavior to become more respectful, loving, and responsible. Logical consequences are recommended to address inappropriate behavior that is in violation of the family guidelines.

CREATING AND COOPERATING WITH FAMILY RULES

INSTRUCTIONS FOR THE PARENTS

Meet as a family group to list all the family rules necessary for the safe, effective, loving, and harmonious functioning of the family unit. Use a brainstorming process, which encourages all family members to participate and considers all suggestions as possible options. Request that rules should be general, short, and stated positively if possible. Record all ideas on a whiteboard or a large sheet of paper.

After all suggestions have been made work together to consolidate the ideas into five or six broad, positive categories (e.g., treat self and others with respect, act responsibly toward self and others, demonstrate unconditional love for all family members).

Example:

Suggested Rule	**Broad Positive Family Guidelines**
Use acceptable vocabulary	
Cooperate with others	
Respect others physically and emotionally	Treat self and others with respect
Tell the truth	
Ask permission to borrow others' belongings	

Keep room clean	
Complete chores	
Be polite while eating	Act responsibly toward self, others, and property
Keep curfew	
Maintain acceptable grades	
Attend church	

Visit grandma once per week

Do random acts of kindness

Play game with little brother

Attend sister's athletic event

Show interest in Mom's activities

Run errands with Dad

Demonstrate unconditional love for all family members

Arrange the list of rules you have brainstormed with your family to fit into several broader categories that are general, positive, and short, and will become your family guidelines.

Suggested Family Rule   **Broad Positive Family Guidelines**

_____

_____

_____   _____

_____

_____

_____

_____

_____

_____   _____

_____

_____

_____   _____

_____

_____

_____

_____
_____
_____   _____
_____
_____
_____
_____
_____
_____   _____
_____
_____
_____

Any future inappropriate behavior that violates one of the broader family guidelines should be considered a rule violation, even though the rule has not been specifically recorded. For example, riding a bike to the store with friends without permission may not have been specified as a family rule; however, it does violate the family guideline of acting responsibly toward self and others, and therefore may be dealt with by a consequence.

Indicate that the consequences for rule violations will be determined to help the child acquire and demonstrate more appropriate behavior that is consistent with the family guidelines. The parent and child may design their own consequences or draw from a suggested list of privileges if appropriate. See the "Using Privileges as Contingencies and Consequences" activity in this Homework Planner.

Review the rules at the next family meeting to gain each member's input and to revise if necessary. Emphasize that the family rules are important to encourage family cooperation and to develop family regard, respect, and responsible behavior.

Section XI

DEPRESSION

CREATING POSITIVE SELF-TALK

GOALS OF THE EXERCISE

1. Identify negative perceptions that have become part of the child's self-talk.
2. Identify the source of the negative self-talk.
3. Identify situations that trigger negative self-talk.
4. Replace negative self-talk with realistic, positive, and affirming statements.

ADDITIONAL HOMEWORK THAT MAY BE APPLICABLE TO FAMILIES COPING WITH DEPRESSION

• Children with Physical Challenges	Strategies for Supporting Our Child with Physical Challenges	Page 100
• Divorce/Separation	Divorce is Not My Fault	Page 142
• Eating Disorder	Modeling Healthy Attitudes about Nutrition, Exercise, and Body Image	Page 156
• Strategies for Teenagers (Ages 13 to 18)	Listening with Empathy	Page 330

ADDITIONAL PROBLEMS THIS EXERCISE MAY BE MOST USEFUL FOR

- Divorce/Separation
- Eating Disorder
- Strategies for Teenagers (Ages 13 to 18)
- Children with Physical Challenges
- Suicide Prevention

SUGGESTIONS FOR USING THIS EXERCISE WITH FAMILIES

Negative comments flippantly made by others can become part of an ongoing litany of personal statements that erode the child's self-confidence and create feelings of inadequacy and depression. The child's negative self-talk can have far-reaching effects on current and future performance and on the capacity to function according to expectations and ability. This activity directs the parents and the child to identify negative self-talk and translate it into optimistic and realistic statements that will encourage personal best performance and the development of healthy self-esteem.

CREATING POSITIVE SELF-TALK

INSTRUCTIONS FOR THE PARENTS

Negative self-talk can influence self-esteem and undermine the child's confidence and his or her courage to attempt new activities and to function according to reasonable expectations and personal ability level. The habit of demeaning oneself using derogatory terms is influenced by name-calling and put-downs from family, peer group, teachers, coaches, and the media. Negative terms, used in anger, as humorous or flippant remarks, or in an attempt to challenge or motivate the child can become part of a negative self-image and can lead to feelings of insecurity, self-doubt, personal loathing, frustration, fear, and depression.

Collaborate with the child to list all of the negative terms that are chronically self-imposed as the result of put-downs, character attacks, and negative humor or sarcasm used by others to describe personal traits, abilities, and overall character. Identify the specific negative self-talk; indicate when it is used and its original source. Remain alert to additional negative statements made by the child throughout the week and add to the list as necessary.

Negative Self-talk	When It Is Used	Source of the Put-down
Examples:		
You dummy.	Whenever I make a mistake	Siblings and friends
I can't hit the broad side of a barn.	Shooting hoops	Comment made by Dad
I can't carry a tune in a basket.	Choir tryouts	Elementary music teacher
_____	_____	_____
_____	_____	_____
_____	_____	_____
_____	_____	_____
_____	_____	_____
_____	_____	_____
_____	_____	_____
_____	_____	_____
_____	_____	_____
_____	_____	_____
_____	_____	_____
_____	_____	_____
_____	_____	_____
_____	_____	_____
_____	_____	_____
_____	_____	_____
_____	_____	_____

Now help the child to develop new ways to soften and eventually eliminate the negative self-talk by evaluating character, ability, and personal traits, and by substituting positive and realistic self-talk terms for negative self-talk. Model for the child the technique of using a compassionate and supportive approach to evaluate oneself. Make sure that the child receives encouragement and recognition for turning negative self-talk into positive, optimistic, and affirming personal statements.

Negative Self-talk	When It Is Used	Positive/Realistic Alternative
Examples:		
I'm so fat; nothing looks good on me.	Trying on new clothes or getting dressed for a special event	My weight is normal for my height; I need to wear styles that flatter my proportions.
I'm too small to play basketball.	During basketball tryouts	I can make the team by concentrating on my shooting and dribbling skills.

MANAGING POSITIVE AND NEGATIVE RELATIONSHIPS

GOALS OF THE EXERCISE

1. Identify significant relationships in the child's life.
2. Evaluate the relationships in terms of positive and negative influences on the child.
3. Determine strategies for supporting positive relationships.
4. Develop and implement methods of defending against the destructive effects of negative relationships.

ADDITIONAL HOMEWORK THAT MAY BE APPLICABLE TO FAMILIES COPING WITH DEPRESSION

- Peer Relationships/Influences

  Social Influences in My Child's Life — Page 203

  Peer Pressures, Values, and Influences — Page 207

- Sexual Responsibility

  Sexual Responsibility and Healthy Self-esteem — Page 258

- Substance Abuse

  Healthy Habits to Support Recovery — Page 343

ADDITIONAL PROBLEMS THIS EXERCISE MAY BE MOST USEFUL FOR

- Conduct Disorder/Delinquent Behavior
- Eating Disorder
- Peer Relationships
- Sexual Responsibility
- Substance Abuse

SUGGESTIONS FOR USING THIS EXERCISE WITH FAMILIES

Children frequently need help in managing the personal relationships that influence their lives. Differentiating relationships that support character development, positive personal choices, and healthy self-esteem from those that create negative influences, self-doubt, and depression is a crucial aspect of positive parenting. This activity helps the parents and child identify significant relationships and determine their positive and negative effects. Strategies are developed to encourage the child to sustain the positive relationships and to mitigate the destructive influences of negative relationships upon behavior, decisions, self-esteem, attitude, and goal setting.

MANAGING POSITIVE AND NEGATIVE RELATIONSHIPS

INSTRUCTIONS FOR THE PARENTS AND THE CHILD

Children of all ages need to learn strategies for managing the positive and negative influences in their lives. Significant relationships with family members, friends, classmates, teachers, coaches, and other role models can have profound effects upon the child, which will remain throughout a lifetime. Through modeling, discussion, and awareness activities parents can help their children to foster and encourage relationships that support the development of character, morals, values, and healthy self-esteem, and to mitigate the harmful effects of toxic relationships.

Brainstorm with the child a list of all the significant relationships that influence daily behavior, decisions, self-esteem, attitudes, and future goals. Then define each association according to the positive or negative influences on the child in the preceding categories. Evaluate each relationship as having an overall negative or positive effect upon the child.

Then, help the child to determine strategies for encouraging positive relationships and discouraging destructive relationships. Ask the child to select one friendship to actively support and sustain and one relationship to defend against.

Brainstorm a list of significant relationships in the child's life and rate them according to the positive or negative influences they have.

Examples:

Positive (+) or Negative (–) Influences of Significant Relationships

Name and Relationship:	Behavior	Decisions	Self-esteem	Attitudes	Future Goals	Overall Influence
Charley (cousin)	–	–	+	–	+	–/+
Allison (older sister)	+	+	+	+	+	+

Positive (+) or Negative (−) Influences of Significant Relationships

Name and Relationship:	Behavior	Decisions	Self-esteem	Attitudes	Future Goals	Overall Influence
_____	_____	_____	_____	_____	_____	_____
_____	_____	_____	_____	_____	_____	_____
_____	_____	_____	_____	_____	_____	_____
_____	_____	_____	_____	_____	_____	_____
_____	_____	_____	_____	_____	_____	_____
_____	_____	_____	_____	_____	_____	_____
_____	_____	_____	_____	_____	_____	_____
_____	_____	_____	_____	_____	_____	_____
_____	_____	_____	_____	_____	_____	_____
_____	_____	_____	_____	_____	_____	_____

Positive (+) or Negative (−) Influences of Significant Relationships

Name and Relationship:	Behavior	Decisions	Self-esteem	Attitudes	Future Goals	Overall Influence
_____	_____	_____	_____	_____	_____	_____
_____	_____	_____	_____	_____	_____	_____
_____	_____	_____	_____	_____	_____	_____
_____	_____	_____	_____	_____	_____	_____
_____	_____	_____	_____	_____	_____	_____
_____	_____	_____	_____	_____	_____	_____
_____	_____	_____	_____	_____	_____	_____
_____	_____	_____	_____	_____	_____	_____
_____	_____	_____	_____	_____	_____	_____
_____	_____	_____	_____	_____	_____	_____

Identify methods of sustaining relationships that contribute to the child's sense of well-being and healthy self-esteem.

Examples:

Phone conversations	Mutual study time
Invite to a family outing	E-mail
Send cards	Collaborate on a project
Arrange a play date	Play a game
Attend an event together	Active listening

Activities to Strengthen Positive Relationships:

Brainstorm strategies that will help the child negate the dangerous, destructive, and/or disturbing influences of negative relationships.

Examples:

Use "I" statements	Share concerns with an empathetic adult
Make new friends	Use conflict resolution strategies
Confront put-downs	Use positive self-talk
Limit time spent together	Refuse to indulge in harmful activities
Develop positive goals for the future	Join a positive and supportive peer group

Methods of Defending Against Negative Relationships:

Choose one relationship to actively support.

Name and relationship: _____

Methods of supporting this positive relationship:

_____   _____

_____   _____

_____   _____

Choose one relationship to actively discourage.

Name and relationship: _____

Methods of defending against the negative effects of this relationship:

_____   _____

_____   _____

_____   _____

Section XII

DIVORCE/SEPARATION

DIVORCE IS NOT MY FAULT

GOALS OF THE EXERCISE

1. Clarify that divorce is an adult decision.
2. Reduce the child's feelings of guilt and/or blame.
3. Identify the many reasons why adults divorce.
4. Help the child gain acceptance of the adult decision to divorce.

ADDITIONAL HOMEWORK THAT MAY BE APPLICABLE TO FAMILIES COPING WITH DIVORCE

• Attention-seeking Behavior	My Love and Trust Support Network	Page 42
• Blended Family	Healing Hurt Feelings	Page 49
• Grief/Loss	Grief and Loss Circle of Support	Page 188
• Depression	Managing Positive and Negative Relationships	Page 134

ADDITIONAL PROBLEMS THIS EXERCISE MAY BE MOST USEFUL FOR

- Blended Family
- Depression
- Grief/Loss
- Poverty-related Issues

SUGGESTIONS FOR USING THIS EXERCISE WITH FAMILIES

Divorce creates feelings of guilt and self-blame in all family members, especially the involved children. When children blame themselves for the divorce it can lead to anger, depression, and unrealistic attempts to reunite the parents. This activity directs the parents to review the common reasons for divorce with the child and to identify and explain the specific reasons for their own decision. The parents take full responsibility, in writing, for the decision to divorce, and the child is exonerated, in writing, from causing the separation or divorce. This will allow the child to reduce feelings of guilt and move on to acceptance of the new family status.

DIVORCE IS NOT MY FAULT

INSTRUCTIONS FOR THE PARENTS AND THE CHILD

Children often assume responsibility for their parents' separation or divorce. This can lead to feelings of guilt, depression, and an inability to move on with their lives. Children who blame themselves for the divorce may focus their emotional energy on manipulating their parents to reunite, rather than accepting the parents' decision to divorce and adjusting to the new family status. All children of divorce need to hear that divorce is an adult decision and is not caused by the children involved.

Meet individually or as co-parents with the child in a quiet, distraction-free setting to take full responsibility for the decision to separate or divorce. Assure the child that the loving relationship with both parents will continue and that you, as parents, will always be involved in the child's life.

Indicate that there are many reasons why parents separate by referring to the following. Brainstorm more reasons why married adults separate and add them to the list. Then, explain in age-appropriate language and specific terms why your separation or divorce is occurring. Remember that it is much healthier for the child to have specific information from you than to rely upon speculation from other family members, friends, or from feelings of self-doubt or blame.

Review the list of reasons adults divorce with your child and add some additional reasons generated by your discussion or your personal situation:

Stress	Money problems
Alcohol or drug usage	Relationship problems
Failure to communicate	Abuse or neglect
Different interests	Different values
Different religions	Extended family conflict
Job pressures	Unemployment
Irresponsible behavior	Unequal distribution of workload
Different social goals	Personal incompatibility

The reasons my parents are separating or divorcing are:

_____

_____

_____

_____

_____

The people responsible for the decision to separate or divorce are:

_____   _____

The children who are not responsible for the decision to separate or divorce are:

_____   _____

_____   _____

_____   _____

_____   _____

ASSUMING OUR PARENTAL RESPONSIBILITIES

GOALS OF THE EXERCISE

1. Identify the family responsibilities of the divorcing parents.
2. Divide the family responsibilities equitably between the parents.
3. Negotiate areas of disagreement relating to ongoing family responsibilities.
4. Maintain a safe and secure lifestyle for all family members after the divorce.

ADDITIONAL HOMEWORK THAT MAY BE APPLICABLE TO FAMILIES COPING WITH DIVORCE

• Character Development	Division of Family Labor	Page 86
	Sharing the Family Resources	Page 90
• Poverty-related Issues	Achieving Family Goals	Page 227
• Spousal Role and Relationship Conflict	Our Evolving Marriage and Spousal Roles	Page 287

ADDITIONAL PROBLEMS THIS EXERCISE MAY BE MOST USEFUL FOR

- Blended Family
- Character Development
- Poverty-related Issues
- Spousal Role and Relationship Conflict

SUGGESTIONS FOR USING THIS EXERCISE WITH FAMILIES

Separation or divorce changes the roles and responsibilities of all family members. Many responsibilities, such as financial support and child care, must be renegotiated so that the separated parents can sustain the physical, social, and emotional well-being of all concerned. The activity directs the parents to record all of the tasks necessary to support themselves and the children after the divorce. The listed responsibilities are then divided between the parents, and a commitment to ongoing support and involvement is obtained. The parents are encouraged to seek guidance from a family counselor or mediator when consensus becomes difficult.

ASSUMING OUR PARENTAL RESPONSIBILITIES

INSTRUCTIONS FOR THE PARENTS AND THE CHILD

Separation or divorce changes the roles and responsibilities of all family members. Many responsibilities such as financial support and child care must be renegotiated so that the separated parents can sustain the physical, social, and emotional well-being of all concerned. Radical changes in lifestyle created by the divorce and lack of parental co-operation to support the needs of the child can lead to serious mental health issues for all involved. Ideally, as parents you will work together to maintain a secure lifestyle for yourselves and the child. Identifying the family responsibilities and dividing them equitably, based upon each parent's ability to contribute, can accomplish this goal.

Begin by listing all of the jobs required to sustain a safe and healthy lifestyle for the child. Then equitably distribute the jobs between each parent. This task will require an ongoing dedication to the welfare of the child. Remember that the child will benefit most from the loving commitment, contributions, and involvement of both parents. An inequitable division of responsibility will hurt both the parents and the involved children in both the short and long term. If the task of dividing the parental responsibilities becomes too difficult or impossible, seek the help of a family counselor or family mediator. All involved parties will benefit greatly if this activity is completed with the utmost focus upon the welfare of the children involved.

Brainstorm typical jobs assumed by divorced or separated parents by adding to the following list:

Financial support	Paying bills	Cooking
Cleaning	Child care	Entertainment
Grocery shopping	Educational support	Attending school activities
Discipline	Religious education	Love and emotional support

Now assign each task to one or both parents. For shared jobs, assign a percentage of the responsibility or a time frame to ensure that the task is completely covered. Begin with the responsibilities that can be easily distributed. If there are jobs or shared responsibilities that cannot be agreed upon, list the job only and seek guidance from your family counselor or mediator. Remember, this will be an ongoing list of assignments to be distributed and redistributed as the children mature and family needs and responsibilities change.

Examples:

Task or Responsibility	Parent Responsible	% or Time of Shared Responsibility
Child care	Both parents	Mom, weekdays; Dad, weekends and Wednesday night
Financial support	Both parents	Dad 60%, Mom 40%

Task or Responsibility	Parent Responsible	% or Time of Shared Responsibility

Task or Responsibility	Parent Responsible	% or Time of Shared Responsibility

Signature of parents: Date:

_____   _____

_____   _____

Section XIII

EATING DISORDER

BEAUTIFUL ON THE INSIDE

GOALS OF THE EXERCISE

1. Identify qualities that constitute character and inner beauty.
2. Identify role models that epitomize high standards of personal character.
3. Recognize the child's developing positive inner qualities.
4. View character development and inner beauty as an ongoing lifelong process.

ADDITIONAL HOMEWORK THAT MAY BE APPLICABLE TO FAMILIES COPING WITH EATING DISORDERS

*   Character Development   Division of Family Labor   Page 86
        Sharing the Family Resources   Page 90
*   Oppositional Defiant Disorder   Family-Approved Media List   Page 198
    (ODD)
*   Peer Relationships/Influences   Peer Pressures, Values, and Influences   Page 207

ADDITIONAL PROBLEMS THIS EXERCISE MAY BE MOST USEFUL FOR

*   Character Development
*   Oppositional Defiant Disorder (ODD)
*   Peer Relationships/Influences
*   Substance Abuse

SUGGESTIONS FOR USING THIS EXERCISE WITH FAMILIES

Eating disorders and other childhood psychological struggles are supported by our media and cultural focus upon superficial and external physical gifts, rather than on the qualities that constitute inner beauty. This activity directs that the parents and child brainstorm those personal assets that create character, healthy self-esteem, compassion, and inner strength. The parents and child, using examples from personal acquaintances and celebrity figures, list role models for positive internal qualities. Both the parents and the child are encouraged to view the acquisition of inner beauty as a lifelong process that should be reviewed frequently to evaluate progress toward future personality and character goals.

BEAUTIFUL ON THE INSIDE

INSTRUCTIONS FOR THE PARENTS AND THE CHILD

Our media and cultural focus upon appearance and superficial qualities can influence children and teens to evaluate themselves in terms of unrealistic, external rather than internal values and character. Physical attractiveness and abilities are subject to change and diminish as we age and societal values transition. However, inner qualities that constitute a person's character will last a lifetime and will contribute to true inner beauty.

Brainstorm a list of inner qualities that create a personality that is loveable, capable, and of high moral character. Focus upon assets attributed to people that contribute, rather than detract, from the well-being of themselves, others, and the larger society. Think of qualities demonstrated by family members, friends, community members, current celebrities, and historical figures. Then create a list of role models that are beautiful on the inside.

Character Assets that Contribute to Inner Beauty:

Examples:

Friendly smile	Responsible behavior	Fun-loving
Compassion	Respect for others	Energetic
Cheerfulness	Carefulness	Active listening
Empathy	Honesty	Loves others unconditionally

Role Models Who Epitomize Inner Beauty

(Include family members, friends, teachers, mentors, community members, historical figures, and celebrities):

Examples:

Mother Teresa	Althea Gibson	Abraham Lincoln
Eleanor Roosevelt	Benjamin Franklin	Gandhi

Finally, work together to establish an ongoing list of those inner qualities that the child currently demonstrates, is in the process of developing, and that will be established in the future. Remember that becoming beautiful on the inside is an unending process that will last a lifetime. As the child matures many qualities in the second and third columns will be moved into the first column. Revisit this list often to reinforce the child and family's commitment to focus on and affirm character development and inner beauty.

My Existing Inner Qualities	Developing Inner Qualities	Future Inner Qualities

MODELING HEALTHY ATTITUDES ABOUT NUTRITION, EXERCISE, AND BODY IMAGE

GOALS OF THE EXERCISE

1. Model positive attitudes toward nutrition, exercise, and body image.
2. Identify negative comments describing personal and others' physical fitness.
3. Reframe negative comments about physical fitness into helpful, positive statements.
4. Agree to support efforts to encourage family health and fitness.

ADDITIONAL HOMEWORK THAT MAY BE APPLICABLE TO FAMILIES COPING WITH EATING DISORDERS

ADDITIONAL PROBLEMS THIS EXERCISE MAY BE MOST USEFUL FOR

- Depression
- Peer Relationships
- Posttraumatic Stress Disorder (PTSD)
- Suicide Prevention

SUGGESTIONS FOR USING THIS EXERCISE WITH FAMILIES

Children develop attitudes about their body image, nutrition, and exercise habits from their parents, significant others, and the media. Parents are often unaware of the profound effect their modeling and negative comments have made until the child develops problems with eating, physical fitness, self-esteem, body image, or peer relationships. This activity directs the parents and child to become aware of comments that are frequently made by family members that reflect positive and negative attitudes about body image and fitness. Negative comments are then reframed into more positive and supportive statements, with the awareness and involvement of all family members.

MODELING HEALTHY ATTITUDES ABOUT NUTRITION, EXERCISE, AND BODY IMAGE

INSTRUCTIONS FOR THE PARENTS AND THE CHILD

Parents' comments about nutrition, exercise, and body image are extremely influential in shaping the child's self-image and attitudes toward eating, physical fitness, and personal health. Parents are often influenced by transitory societal and media norms that are harmful to the child's undeveloped and malleable self-concept. Flippant remarks that are uttered in a joking and self-deprecating manner can have serious impact upon children, who view their parents' statements as the ultimate authority.

Review all comments made by family members regarding their own and others' physical appearance and fitness for one week. Begin to replace negative with positive comments in your daily self-talk and comments to others. Encourage other family members to do the same. You can make a game of it and actually influence a more positive self-concept and personal perception of body image for yourself and the entire family.

Examples:

Comment	Source	Positive	Negative
"I hate my legs, they're so fat."	Sister		X
"I'll never lose this weight."	Dad		X
"I always feel great after my walk."	Mom	X	

Weekly record of comments made regarding eating habits, body image, and exercise:

Comment	Source	Positive	Negative

Comment	Source	Positive	Negative

Brainstorm ways of turning negative comments about nutrition, body image, and health habits into positive or supportive statements that can help family members accept and appreciate their bodies and adopt habits that will contribute to personal health, happiness, and an energetic, fulfilling lifestyle.

Examples:

Negative Comment	Positive Alternative Comment
"My legs are so fat."	"My legs are strong and normal for my height."
"I'll never lose that weight."	"I need to start walking with my wife."

Negative Comment	Positive Alternative Comment

Negative Comment	Positive Alternative Comment

Be alert on a daily basis for comments that detract from positive body image and healthy self-esteem. Help all family members to reframe negative, hurtful statements into positive alternative comments. Be open to the encouragement and support offered by others and thank them for their efforts to develop a more positive and realistic attitude toward nutrition, exercise, and body image. Ask each family member to sign a pledge to eliminate negative comments from the family repertoire.

I pledge my efforts to turn my own and our family's negative talk about body image and fitness into positive, productive statements.

_____   _____

_____   _____

_____   _____

_____   _____

Section XIV

GIFTED/TALENTED

TEACHING RESPONSIBILITY

GOALS OF THE EXERCISE

1. Determine age-appropriate tasks that can be completed by the child.
2. List consequences to be used when assigned tasks have not been completed.
3. Encourage the child to make responsible choices and demonstrate appropriate behavior.
4. Use a four-step process to teach responsibility.

ADDITIONAL HOMEWORK THAT MAY BE APPLICABLE TO TEACHING RESPONSIBILITY

• Attention-seeking Behavior	Family Job Support Checklist	Page 37
• Strategies for Preschoolers (Ages Birth to 6)	Helping My Child Develop Responsible Behavior	Page 305
• Strategies for Children (Ages 7 to 12)	Problem-solving Worksheet	Page 323
• Strategies for Teenagers (Ages 13 to 18)	Earning Privileges and Freedoms	Page 335

ADDITIONAL PROBLEMS THIS EXERCISE MAY BE MOST USEFUL FOR

- Attention-seeking Behavior
- Strategies for Preschoolers
- Strategies for Children
- Strategies for Teenagers

SUGGESTIONS FOR USING THIS EXERCISE WITH FAMILIES

Teaching children to become responsible begins with assigning tasks and chores in the home. This activity uses a four-step process defined by Cline and Fay in *Parenting with Love and Logic* (Navpress, 1990): (1) give the child a manageable task; (2) hope that the child "blows" it; (3) let equal parts of consequence and empathy do the teaching; (4) give the same task again. The parents and child are asked to brainstorm a list of age appropriate tasks for the child to complete and a list of consequences to use if the task is not accomplished appropriately. The four-step process is then implemented regularly to help the child make responsible choices and demonstrate appropriate behavior.

TEACHING RESPONSIBILITY

INSTRUCTIONS FOR THE PARENTS AND THE CHILD

Children learn responsibility by completing tasks and chores and by participating in the family's workload. It is unrealistic to expect the child to perform responsibly in school and in adulthood when task completion and helpful behavior has not been encouraged from an early age in the home. Self-esteem is enhanced when the child considers the positive efforts that have been made and develops pride and a sense of accomplishment throughout childhood and adolescence. Cline and Fay outline four steps to teach responsibility to children in their book *Parenting with Love and Logic:* (1) give the child a manageable task; (2) hope that the child "blows" it; (3) let equal parts of consequence and empathy do the teaching; (4) give the same task again. Use this activity repeatedly to teach children of all ages that responsible behavior contributes to a successful life and a sense of wellbeing.

Begin by brainstorming age-appropriate tasks that can be accomplished by the child (e.g., pick up toys, wash dishes, feed dog, baby-sit, clean room, complete homework). Then, create a list of possible consequences to use when responsible behavior has not been demonstrated (e.g., loss of TV time, computer, toys or car, restricted curfew, earlier bedtime, miss fun activities). Use the tasks and consequences lists to implement the four-step process and to teach the child to make responsible choices and to demonstrate appropriate behavior.

Work together to create a list of age-appropriate tasks for the child that can be used to teach responsibility.

Brainstorm a list of natural or logical consequences.

Implement the four-step process to teach responsibility.

1. Choose a task for the child to complete.

    _____

2. Evaluate the child's effort in terms of willingness to cooperate, task completion, and quality of the work.

    _____

3. Congratulate the child on a job well done if the task has been completed effectively; if not, determine a consequence, to be delivered with empathy, to teach responsible decision-making (e.g., "So sorry, no TV until the homework is complete").

    _____

4. Give the same task again to check for learning (e.g., child is allowed to watch TV next day after homework is completed).

    _____

PROCEDURES FOR MEALS, BEDTIME, AND THE MORNING ROUTINE

GOALS OF THE EXERCISE

1. Establish specific and sequential procedures for meals, bedtime, and the morning routine.
2. List natural and logical consequences for noncompliance of each procedure.
3. Reduce the stress and frustration involved in important family activities.
4. Teach responsible behavior during crucial family routines.

ADDITIONAL HOMEWORK THAT MAY BE APPLICABLE TO ESTABLISHING FAMILY ROUTINES

• Attention-Deficit/ Hyperactivity Disorder (ADHD)	Family Problem Resolution Worksheet	Page 29
• Conduct Disorder/Delinquent Behavior	Replacing Noncompliance with Compliance and Cooperation	Page 109
• Dependent Children/ Overprotective Parent	Creating and Cooperating with Family Rules	Page 124
• School Adjustment Difficulties	Organizing for the School Day	Page 248

ADDITIONAL PROBLEMS THIS EXERCISE MAY BE MOST USEFUL FOR

- Attention-Deficit/Hyperactivity Disorder (ADHD)
- Conduct Disorder/Delinquent Behavior
- Dependent Children/Overprotective Parent
- School Adjustment Difficulties

SUGGESTIONS FOR USING THIS EXERCISE WITH FAMILIES

By establishing specific and sequential procedures, parents can reduce conflict and enhance the cooperative efforts of their children during meals, bedtime, and the morning routine. This activity guides the parents and child to determine the steps required for each activity and to list possible consequences for failure to comply with each procedure. The process will help the child feel included in determining the necessary behavior required for successful participation in each routine.

PROCEDURES FOR MEALS, BEDTIME, AND THE MORNING ROUTINE

INSTRUCTIONS FOR THE PARENTS AND THE CHILD

Procedures help children to develop appropriate, predictable, and consistent behavior during important and often stressful family routines. Arguing and manipulation can be avoided during meals, bedtime, and in the morning by establishing the steps necessary to successfully complete each activity. Look over the examples that follow of some procedures involved in accomplishing successful family meals, bedtime, and the morning routine. Then collaborate to brainstorm the sequential steps required in your particular family circumstances, and include the natural and logical consequences which will occur if the steps are not appropriately completed. Revise the procedures for each routine as family needs and circumstances change.

Steps and Consequences Involved in a Successful Morning Routine

Examples:

Steps Necessary for the Morning Routine	Natural and Logical Consequences for Noncompliance
Lay out school clothes the night before	Rushing to find clothes in the morning
Organize materials needed for school the night before	Rushing to find materials in the morning
Shower the night before	Shower in morning or forget shower
Set alarm clock	Problem waking up on time
Go to bed at 9:00	Sleepy in the morning
Wake up when alarm rings	Late start in morning, no time for breakfast
Wash, dress, comb hair	Appear messy
Eat breakfast	Hungry in school, no food until lunch
Leave for school on time	Late for school, suffer school-imposed consequences, and get up earlier the next morning to ensure on-time arrival

Steps and Consequences Involved in a Successful Morning Routine

Steps Necessary for the Morning Routine	Natural and Logical Consequences for Noncompliance

Steps and Consequences Involved in a Successful Bedtime Routine

Examples:

Steps Necessary for the Bedtime Routine	Natural and Logical Consequences for Noncompliance
Bath or shower	Lose quiet time
Brush teeth	Lose quiet time
Put on pajamas	Lose quiet time
Gather school materials	Feel rushed in morning
Lay out school clothes	Feel rushed in morning
Quiet time (e.g., read story, listen to music, say prayers)	Problem falling asleep
Use toilet, get drink of water	Problem falling asleep
Set alarm clock	Problem waking up in morning
Go to bed on time	Start bedtime routine earlier the next night and/or earlier bedtime

Steps and Consequences Involved in a Successful Bedtime Routine

Steps Necessary for the Bedtime Routine	Natural and Logical Consequences for Noncompliance

Steps and Consequences Involved in Creating Successful and Enjoyable Family Meals

Examples:

Steps Necessary for Enjoyable Family Meals	Natural and Logical Consequences for Noncompliance
Plan family meals in advance	Disorganized food preparation
Determine time for family meal	Confusion about meal time
Assist in meal preparation	Extra cleanup duties
Sit down at table on time with the family	Extra meal preparation duties the next night
No TV allowed during meal	TV interferes with family cohesion
Eat an appropriate amount of food	No dessert or evening snacks
Remain seated during entire meal	Excused to time-out area
Use polite table manners	Excused to time-out area
Thank the cook for the meal preparation	Extra cleanup duties assigned
Help with the cleanup	Extra meal preparation duties the next night

Steps and Consequences Involved in Creating Successful and Enjoyable Family Meals

Steps Necessary for Enjoyable Family Meals	Natural and Logical Consequences for Noncompliance

GRANDPARENTING STRATEGIES

PARENTS' RULES VERSUS GRANDPARENTS' RULES

GOALS OF THE EXERCISE

1. Parents and grandparents establish specific rules for the grandchildren in each setting.
2. Compare the rules established by the parents and grandparents.
3. Assist the grandchildren in adjusting to various rules in different settings.
4. Parents and grandparents establish limits based on their personal values and circumstances.

ADDITIONAL HOMEWORK THAT MAY BE APPLICABLE TO STRATEGIES FOR GRANDPARENTS

• Attention-seeking Behavior	My Love and Trust Support Network	Page 37
• Gifted/Talented	Procedures for Meals, Bedtime, and the Morning Routine	Page 165
• Poverty-related Issues	Different Rules for Home and School	Page 231
• Spousal Role and Relationship Conflict	Our Evolving Marriage and Spousal Roles	Page 287

ADDITIONAL PROBLEMS THIS EXERCISE MAY BE MOST USEFUL FOR

- Attention-seeking Behavior
- Gifted/Talented
- Poverty-related Issues
- Spousal Role and Relationship Conflict

SUGGESTIONS FOR USING THIS EXERCISE WITH FAMILIES

Grandparents and parents can reduce the confusion caused by different rules by clearly stating their individual limits for the grandchildren. This activity guides the parents and grandparents to involve the grandchildren in defining the rules established in each setting or circumstance and then to identify those rules that are similar and those that are different. The activity helps the grandchildren to adjust to the different sets of rules and prepares them for the different regulations they will experience in school, church, and community. The parents and grandparents are encouraged to accept their personal differences in values and circumstances that may be reflected in the rules they establish for the grandchildren.

PARENTS' RULES VERSUS GRANDPARENTS' RULES

INSTRUCTIONS FOR THE GRANDPARENTS AND THE PARENTS

Rules established in the grandparent's home may vary substantially or just slightly from the rules established by the parents. Children can adjust to two or more sets of rules if they are clearly stated and identified as a "parent's rule" or a "grandparent's rule." As the children mature they will be exposed to even more sets of rules at school, church, and in the homes of their friends. It is helpful for them to understand that while some rules are universal, others are tied to a particular setting or circumstance.

Brainstorm a list of rules that are established in the parents' and the grandparents' home. Involve the grandchildren in this process. Consider rules for meals, bedtime, respecting property, polite and helpful behavior, and other important areas of functioning. Try to state the rules in the positive rather than using a lot of "don'ts" (e.g., leave your muddy shoes at the door versus don't track mud on the kitchen floor). The rules in each setting will change as the children grow and circumstances change. Consider the initial list the beginning of a process that will continue until the grandchildren are adults and establishing rules in their own homes.

Create a list of the important rules established by the parents.

Parents' Rules

Create a list of the important rules established by the grandparents.

Grandparents' Rules

Now consider which rules are similar in both environments.

Parents' Rules	Grandparents' Rules

List the rules that are different in each home.

Parents' Rules	Grandparents' Rules

PERSONAL BOUNDARIES FOR INTERACTION WITH THE GRANDCHILDREN

GOALS OF THE EXERCISE

1. Record specific boundaries and expectations held by the grandparents, parents, and grandchildren.
2. Communicate expectations and boundaries to the involved family members.
3. Recognize and respect the expectations and personal boundaries of the involved family members.
4. Review and revise expectations and personal boundaries as family circumstances change.

ADDITIONAL HOMEWORK THAT MAY BE APPLICABLE TO STRATEGIES FOR GRANDPARENTS

• Prenatal Parenting Preparation	Creating a Family-Friendly Lifestyle	Page 238
	Bonding with Our Prenatal Baby	Page 242
• Spousal Role and Relationship Conflict	Our Evolving Marriage and Spousal Roles	Page 287
• Strategies for Teenagers (Ages 13 to 18)	Listening with Empathy	Page 330

ADDITIONAL PROBLEMS THIS EXERCISE MAY BE MOST USEFUL FOR

- Prenatal Parenting Preparation
- Poverty-related Issues
- Spousal Role and Relationship Conflict
- Strategies for Teenagers

SUGGESTIONS FOR USING THIS EXERCISE WITH FAMILIES

By clearly defining personal boundaries and intentions the grandparents, parents, and grandchildren can interact in harmonious and loving ways, and avoid hurt feelings caused by lack of communication and respect for one another's expectations. This activity directs the grandparents, parents, and grandchildren, if age appropriate, to record their personal guidelines for establishing a positive relationship with one another. The guidelines are acknowledged and reviewed at a later date to determine which expectations and boundaries are being met and which need to be respected more fully.

PERSONAL BOUNDARIES FOR INTERACTION WITH THE GRANDCHILDREN

INSTRUCTIONS FOR THE GRANDPARENTS AND THE PARENTS

Parents and grandparents may have very different ideas, expectations, and boundaries for interaction with the grandchildren. Parents may expect the unlimited availability of *their* parents to baby-sit, provide transportation, or even to supply support and housing accommodations, while the grandparents wish to be involved but not constantly on call. Or, the grandparents may desire constant interaction and involvement with their grandchildren, while the parents prefer a less intense relationship between their own parents and their children.

Establishing ideal guidelines for the grandparents, parents, and grandchildren requires that the expectations of each be specifically stated and then communicated with one another. Most grandparents want to be lovingly involved with their grandchildren while not giving up their own routines and lifestyle. Parents usually encourage positive interaction between their parents and the children but want to maintain control of the major decisions. The grandchildren are most often very pleased with the relationship they enjoy with their grandparents but may wish more or less involvement. Problems occur when personal boundaries and expectations are not established, communicated, and respected.

Work together as grandparents, parents, and grandchildren, if age-appropriate, to avoid miscommunication, disappointment, and frustration, by clearly stating the boundaries you each have for interaction with the grandchildren. Consider the obvious and the more hidden expectations and desires you have held over the years. Remember that even though every expectation may not be satisfied, each one should be recorded and shared. All personal boundaries should be respected and observed whenever possible.

Share all expectations with one another and discuss how to create a working arrangement for a positive and loving relationship, to be established among the parents, grandparents, and grandchildren. Revisit the boundaries and expectations periodically as the children grow and circumstances change. Communicate the personal boundaries frequently, and come to consensuses about which boundaries are being accommodated and which need to be addressed and respected more vigorously.

Record all personal boundaries and expectations held by the grandparents.

Examples:

| I will be happy to baby-sit when asked in advance and my schedule permits. |
| I want to spend some quality time with the grandchildren during birthdays and holidays as well as on a regular weekly basis. |

Record all personal boundaries and expectations held by the parents.

Examples:

Please call before you come over.
Transport the kids to soccer once per week.

Record all personal boundaries and expectations held by the grandchildren.

Examples:

Attend my soccer games.
Spend time with me once per week or more.

The boundaries and expectations were shared on

Date: _____

By:

Grandparents:

_____   _____

Parents:

_____   _____

Grandchildren:

_____   _____

_____   _____

Boundaries that are being respected:

Boundaries that need to be addressed and respected more fully:

We will review our boundaries and expectations again on:

Date: _____

Section XVI

GRIEF/LOSS

MONITORING OUR REACTIONS TO CHANGE AND LOSS

GOALS OF THE EXERCISE

1. View grief as a process that evolves through several stages.
2. Differentiate between minor and significant losses.
3. Recognize which stage of grief and loss is being experienced.
4. View potential recovery from grief in optimistic terms.

ADDITIONAL HOMEWORK THAT MAY BE APPLICABLE TO FAMILIES EXPERIENCING GRIEF AND LOSS

• Posttraumatic Stress Disorder (PTSD)	Reframing Our Worries	Page 216
• Strategies for Teenagers (Ages 13 to 18)	Listening with Empathy	Page 330
• Substance Abuse	Healthy Habits to Support Recovery	Page 343
• Suicide Prevention	Heart-to-Heart Smart Talks	Page 354

ADDITIONAL PROBLEMS THIS EXERCISE MAY BE MOST USEFUL FOR

- Depression
- Divorce
- Posttraumatic Stress Disorder (PTSD)
- Strategies for Teenagers
- Substance Abuse

SUGGESTIONS FOR USING THIS EXERCISE WITH FAMILIES

This activity will help the family develop a definition of grief and describe the personal feelings linked to the various stages of the grieving process. Family members are asked to record feelings already experienced and to predict how those feelings will change as time passes and acceptance and adjustment occur. The family then records some positive memories prior to the loss by drawing pictures or pasting photos of positive family experiences. The exercise is designed to give the parents and children hope and optimism for the future while continuing to value the positive memories of the past.

MONITORING OUR REACTIONS TO CHANGE AND LOSS

INSTRUCTIONS FOR THE PARENTS AND THE CHILD

Grief is often defined as a personal reaction to a change or loss. Each little change in our lives means that we experience some discomfort and frustration. As we begin to accept what has happened our feelings adjust, and we learn to live with the change and feel better about the loss that the change created. When a significant change or loss occurs, (e.g., divorce, death, serious injury, illness) the feelings we experience are much stronger and the time it takes to recover is longer. But the process is the same. At first we feel devastated, sad, angry, and powerless, but slowly we begin to adjust to the change and our feelings become less painful and more optimistic. Eventually, we are able to enjoy our lives again and experience happy and enthusiastic feelings. However, the significant loss will always remain in our memories as a bittersweet reminder of that time in our lives which will never again be the same.

Work together as a family to complete the following statements. Share your feelings with one another and record the different reactions of each family member. If your family has just experienced a significant loss, complete only as much of this activity as is appropriate. If the loss occurred just a few weeks or months ago, skip number 4 and go on to items 5 through 7. After you have completed the questions, draw pictures or paste photos of pleasant memories and family experiences before the change or loss occurred. The pictures can be selected or drawn together or individually to remember the family prior to the loss.

1. Some people say that each change in our life creates grief or a feeling of loss.

    For our family, grief means:

    _____

    _____

    _____

    _____

    _____

    _____

    _____

2.   When we first learned about the loss, we felt:

_____

_____

_____

_____

3.   A few weeks later we felt:

_____

_____

_____

_____

4.   After several months we felt:

_____

_____

_____

_____

5.   Now, after _____ (weeks, months, or years) we feel:

_____

_____

_____

_____

6.   Five years from now we may feel:

_____

_____

_____

_____

7.   But we will always remember:

_____

_____

_____

_____

8.   Draw one or more pictures or paste photos of pleasant memories you have of your family prior to the change or loss.

9.   Describe what is happening in the photo or picture.

_____

_____

_____

_____

GRIEF AND LOSS CIRCLE OF SUPPORT

GOALS OF THE EXERCISE

1. Identify sources of comfort within the family, school, work environment, and community.
2. Dispel feelings of loneliness, helplessness, and/or hopelessness.
3. Recognize empathetic gestures from others that have been helpful in dealing with the grief.
4. Extend acts of kindness and support to others who are experiencing grief.

ADDITIONAL HOMEWORK THAT MAY BE APPLICABLE TO FAMILIES EXPERIENCING GRIEF AND LOSS

• Blended Family	Healing Hurt Feelings	Page 49
• Children with Physical Challenges	Strategies for Supporting Our Child with Physical Challenges	Page 100
• Depression	Creating Positive Self-Talk	Page 130
• Posttraumatic Stress Disorder (PTSD)	Physical Receptors of Stress	Page 220

ADDITIONAL PROBLEMS THIS EXERCISE MAY BE MOST USEFUL FOR

- Blended Family
- Depression
- Divorce
- Posttraumatic Stress Disorder (PTSD)
- Substance Abuse

SUGGESTIONS FOR USING THIS EXERCISE WITH FAMILIES

Children and adults who are grieving often feel isolated, helpless, and/or hopeless. They may believe that no one can help them cope with their overwhelming feelings of devastation and loss. This activity directs the parents and children to identify all acts of kindness and encouragement that have been offered from friends, family, and community members. Family members will begin to use the strength and empathy of others to shore up their own ability to cope with the despair and doubts created by the loss. After the healing process has begun, family members are asked to list supportive gestures they could extend to others who are grieving, thus completing the grief and loss circle of support.

GRIEF AND LOSS CIRCLE OF SUPPORT

INSTRUCTIONS FOR THE PARENTS AND THE CHILD

Although grief can create feelings of loneliness and despair, it can also inspire many acts of caring, encouragement, love, and support. By recognizing the family's support system and identifying the uplifting gestures extended by family, fellow workers, the child's school, friends, faith-based groups, and community, parents and children can begin to feel less helpless and hopeless and more optimistic about their ability to cope with grief.

Begin a list of all the gestures that have provided comfort and caring during your time of grief and loss. Include all acts of kindness from the smallest to the largest deed. Name the person or group who has extended the gesture and the person or persons who have received the support. The list should be an extensive record of positive interventions from the family's support system. After the ongoing list has been established, refer to it frequently, either individually or during a family meeting, and discuss how the offerings of encouragement and caring have helped each family member deal with personal grief.

After the healing process has begun and family members are feeling stronger, consider various acts of kindness and support that can be extended to others dealing with the pain of grief and loss. Both parents and children will discover that through the process of offering empathy, caring, and encouragement to others in need, they will overcome the devastation of their own grief and loss.

Examples:

Act of Kindness and Support	Person or Group Extending the Support	Family Member Receiving the Support
Grief counseling for family	Pastor at church	All family members
Reading stories about grief	Grandma	David and Sarah
Bringing food for evening meals	Friends from work	All family members

Act of Kindness and Support	Person or Group Extending the Support	Family Member Receiving the Support

ACTS OF ENCOURAGEMENT AND KINDNESS WE COULD EXTEND TO OTHERS EXPERIENCING GRIEF AND LOSS

Examples:

Act of Support	Family Member Offering the Support
Invite friends whose parents are divorcing to a sleepover	David and Sarah
Visit Aunt Betty who is recovering from surgery	Mom and Dad

Act of Support	Family Member Offering the Support

Section XVII

OPPOSITIONAL DEFIANT DISORDER (ODD)

PLANNING FOR DISRUPTIVE BEHAVIOR

GOALS OF THE EXERCISE

1. Plan ahead for effective management of the child's chronic inappropriate behavior.
2. Remain calm when confronted by the child's oppositional and defiant behavior.
3. Use constructive disciplinary strategies to reduce chronic negative behavior.
4. Evaluate the discipline strategies used and revise if necessary.

ADDITIONAL HOMEWORK THAT MAY BE APPLICABLE TO FAMILIES EXPERIENCING OPPOSITIONAL DEFIANT BEHAVIOR

• Bonding/Attachment Issues	The Behavior Progress Chart	Page 64
• Conduct Disorder/ Delinquent Behavior	Replacing Noncompliance with Compliance and Cooperation	Page 109
	Using Privileges as Contingencies and Consequences	Page 114
• Dependent Children/ Overprotective Parent	Overprotective Parent versus Positive Parent	Page 120
• Gifted/Talented	Teaching Responsibility	Page 162

ADDITIONAL PROBLEMS THIS EXERCISE MAY BE MOST USEFUL FOR

- Attention-Deficit/Hyperactivity Disorder (ADHD)
- Bonding/Attachment Issues
- Conduct Disorder
- Dependent Children/Overprotective Parent
- Gifted/Talented

SUGGESTIONS FOR USING THIS EXERCISE WITH FAMILIES

Parents often feel frustrated and overwhelmed by the child's chronic negative behavior, rather than viewing it as an opportunity to prepare ahead for its inevitable reoccurrence. This activity guides the parents to identify the child's current chronic negative behaviors and to create a management plan that allows them to remain calm and constructive while disciplining the behavior and helping the child acquire more appropriate methods of functioning. After implementation the plan is evaluated to determine the effectiveness of the parent's delivery, the child's response, and the overall results of the strategies used. Strategies to deal with future occurrences of the behavior are selected, if necessary.

PLANNING FOR DISRUPTIVE BEHAVIOR

INSTRUCTIONS FOR THE PARENTS

Chronic negative and oppositional behavior from a child can be extremely frustrating and overwhelming if effective management techniques have not been established in advance. Negative behavior can be even more discouraging for parents who have tried various discipline strategies without success. However, one positive aspect of chronic misbehavior is that it will occur again and again, thus giving the parents many opportunities to respond with positive and effective discipline strategies.

The first rule in discouraging inappropriate behavior is to remain very calm. The oppositional child is expecting the parent to get angry; therefore, a calm response is confusing and unsettling. Anger contributes to the problem, whereas a calm response demonstrates that the parent is in control emotionally and is able to deal with the problem in a constructive manner. Being prepared with a strategy to deal with the unwanted behavior enhances the parent's ability to remain calm and solution-oriented while dealing with the chronic oppositional and defiant behavior. Follow these steps to establish a viable plan to deal with the child's inappropriate behavior.

1. Brainstorm behaviors that the child demonstrates on a regular basis.

    Examples:

Hits sister	Won't pick up toys	Breaks curfew
Refuses to do homework	Disrespectful to Mother	Skips school

    Our child's current chronic misbehavior includes:

2. Review the following list of disciplinary interventions with your counselor to determine which interventions are most useful in various situations. Additional strategies from you or the counselor can be added in the spaces provided.

Effective interventions for eliminating inappropriate behavior:

Defined Choices	Broken Record	Logical Consequences
Natural consequences	Enforceable contingencies	Close parental monitoring
Describe the expected behavior	Four steps to responsibility (see Teaching Responsibility Act)	Encouragement and can-do statements
Reflective listening	Time out	Child makes restitution
Say "you fix it or I'll fix it"	Affirmations	Restricted privileges
Let child create a plan	Reduced curfew	Earlier bedtime
Ask "how can I help?"	Ignore the behavior	I-statements
Select a chore from a chore list	Change the child's location	Remove the problematic object
Self-monitoring		

3. Now create a behavior plan that will help you remain calm and constructive when dealing with your child's chronic negative behavior.

   1. Select one target behavior to eliminate.

   _____

   _____

   2. Select an intervention or consequence that will encourage the child to behave more appropriately.

   _____

   _____

3. State exactly how you will explain the intervention to the child. Don't lecture. Use as few words as possible and let the consequence teach the lesson to the child.

_____

_____

_____

_____

4. Observe and record the child's response. You may have to wait until the next time the circumstance repeats itself to fully determine the child's total response.

_____

_____

_____

_____

5. Evaluate your management of the disciplinary intervention.

_____

_____

_____

_____

6. Evaluate the intervention, and select a different or additional intervention for the next occurrence of the inappropriate behavior, if necessary.

_____

_____

_____

_____

FAMILY-APPROVED MEDIA LIST

GOALS OF THE EXERCISE

1. Limit the child's exposure to TV, movies, computer, and video games.
2. Create an approved list of TV and video programs for the child to view.
3. Engage in activities that promote creativity, learning, and positive interaction among family members.
4. Actively involve the child in evaluating the media viewed by the family.

ADDITIONAL HOMEWORK THAT MAY BE APPLICABLE TO FAMILIES EXPERIENCING OPPOSITIONAL DEFIANT BEHAVIOR

ADDITIONAL PROBLEMS THIS EXERCISE MAY BE MOST USEFUL FOR

- Peer Relationships/Influences
- Poverty-related Issues
- Conduct Disorder
- Sexual Responsibility
- Strategies for Teenagers

SUGGESTIONS FOR USING THIS EXERCISE WITH FAMILIES

Overexposure to the electronic media, including TV, videos, and the computer, can limit the child's ability to learn, interact, and develop responsible behavior. Parents can regain family time and rebuild positive family relationships by limiting their own and their children's media consumption and by restricting media viewing to an approved list. This activity directs the parents to determine a maximum amount of time allowed for media exposure and to involve the child in developing a list of approved media programs. The child can earn additional media time by completing chores, improving school performance, and engaging in appropriate, cooperative behavior.

FAMILY-APPROVED MEDIA LIST

INSTRUCTIONS FOR THE PARENTS

Limiting electronic media exposure is helpful for all children, and is critical for children experiencing behavioral and emotional challenges. Reducing the time spent watching TV or videos, listening to the radio, surfing the Internet, and playing computer or other electronic games allows the child to develop healthier, more stimulating interests, such as reading, constructing, inventing, cooking, creating, interacting, and engaging in his or her own and collaborative musical and artistic experiences.

Begin by determining, as a family, the amount of time per day to be allowed for media consumption. This will depend upon the child's age, maturity, level of responsibility, and self-esteem, but should be limited to one to two hours per day or less. It is essential that the parents limit their own exposure and engage in other more interesting and productive activities so as to support the family commitment to a reduced level of electronic and media consumption.

Agree as a family to restrict TV and video viewing to a family approved list. This list is to be determined by the parents with input from each child, and should reflect the family values for civility, language, character, tolerance, and respect. The parents should monitor all computer time and Internet access.

New TV programs and videos can be added only by joint consent of the parents and the petitioning child and should be previewed together and discussed before approval. Additional time for viewing approved programs or using the computer and Internet can be earned by cooperative behavior, improved school performance, or by completing additional chores.

Complete the statements below to create your family-approved media policy.

1. Our family has agreed to limit all electronic media consumption to _____ hours per day, or _____ hours per week.

2. Our family has approved the following programs for viewing. Additional programs may be added only after previewing, discussion, and consensus of the parents and the child.

3. Additional media time can be earned in the following ways.

   Examples:

Activity or Behavior	Time Earned	Activity or Behavior	Time Earned
Small chores	10 min./wk.	Large chores	30 min./wk.
Baby-sit	30 min./wk.	Weekly homework completed	30 min./wk.
Report card improvement	60 min./wk.	No swearing for one week	60 min./wk.

Section XVIII

PEER RELATIONSHIPS/INFLUENCES

SOCIAL INFLUENCES IN MY CHILD'S LIFE

GOALS OF THE EXERCISE

1. Identify significant role models in the child's life.
2. Recognize the longlasting influence parents have on the child's personality development.
3. Differentiate positive from negative role models.
4. Reduce the influence of negative role models upon the child's attitude and behavior.

ADDITIONAL HOMEWORK THAT MAY BE APPLICABLE TO PEER RELATIONSHIP ISSUES

• Attention-seeking Behavior	My Love and Trust Support Network	Page 42
• Blended Family	Unique Roles in Our Blended Family	Page 53
• Depression	Managing Positive and Negative Relationships	Page 134
• Eating Disorder	Modeling Healthy Attitudes about Nutrition, Exercise, and Body Image	Page 156

ADDITIONAL PROBLEMS THIS EXERCISE MAY BE MOST USEFUL FOR

- Attention-seeking Behavior
- Blended Family
- Depression
- Eating Disorder
- Strategies for Teenagers

SUGGESTIONS FOR USING THIS EXERCISE WITH FAMILIES

Families often fail to recognize the powerful influence that role models have upon the child from a very early age. Some role models exert only temporary influence while others shape the child's personality development and future quality of life. The activity guides the parents and the child, if age appropriate, to list the significant others that control some of the child's decisions, behavior, and opinions. This identification process brings the role models' influence to the conscious level where it can be evaluated and accepted as a positive or rejected as a negative aspect in the child's life. The parents are encouraged to maintain an ongoing record of significant others in the child's life during all of the developmental years from birth to early adulthood.

SOCIAL INFLUENCES IN MY CHILD'S LIFE

INSTRUCTIONS FOR THE PARENTS AND THE CHILD

Children are influenced by family and social role models from the time they are able to observe the actions of others. An infant will smile in response to the parent's smile, a toddler wants to use a spoon or fork, elementary children emulate fictional figures, and teens identify with celebrities from pop culture. Some of the child's role models will have a lasting effect upon self-esteem, personality development, and future goal-setting, while others exert only minor and temporary influence. Often both parents and the child are unaware of the effects that significant role models are having upon the child's current and future lifestyles. It is helpful to thoughtfully analyze the importance of role models in the child's life and to determine their positive or negative influences.

Brainstorm, with the child if age-appropriate, a list of people who significantly influence the child's behavior, attitude, personality development, and decision-making. Include family members, peer group, teachers, mentors, fictional characters, and celebrities. Remember that you as parents and other close family members will have the primary responsibility of shaping the child's personality growth and development.

Rate each role model's relationship with the child as being supportive or nonsupportive and temporary or longlasting. Involve children 12 and older in the activity so they can become aware of the considerable power role models have in their lives. Parents of children under 12 should complete the activity alone to increase their awareness of the influence they and others have in shaping the child's personality.

The process of identifying specific role models will help to regulate their influence and power in the child's life. Both parents and child may want to encourage those relationships that are positive and supportive and eliminate or reduce the influence of those that are negatively affecting the child's behavior and attitude. Continue adding to the list as the child matures, to create an ongoing record of significant others in the child's life.

Examples:

Child's Name and Age	Role Model's Name and Relationship	Supportive/ Nonsupportive	Temporary/ Longlasting
Theresa 2	Mother	Supportive	Longlasting
	Father	Supportive	Longlasting
Theresa 13	Mr. Brown (coach)	Supportive	Longlasting
	James (friend)	Nonsupportive	Temporary
	Britney Spears	Nonsupportive	Temporary

Child's Name and Age	Role Model's Name and Relationship	Supportive/ Nonsupportive	Temporary/ Longlasting

PEER PRESSURES, VALUES, AND INFLUENCES

GOALS OF THE EXERCISE

1. Analyze peer pressure from the child's and the parents' perspectives.
2. Initiate ongoing discussions about peer influences in the child's life.
3. Monitor ongoing peer group values, expectations, and activities.
4. Reduce negative peer group pressures on the child.

ADDITIONAL HOMEWORK THAT MAY BE APPLICABLE TO PEER GROUP INFLUENCES

• Poverty-related Issues	Different Rules for Home and School	Page 231
• Sexual Responsibility	My Personal Sexual Responsibility Code	Page 262
• Substance Abuse	Healthy Habits to Support Recovery	Page 343
• Suicide Prevention	Heart-to-Heart Smart Talks	Page 354

ADDITIONAL PROBLEMS THIS EXERCISE MAY BE MOST USEFUL FOR

- Sexual Responsibility
- Substance Abuse
- Eating Disorder
- Strategies for Teenagers

SUGGESTIONS FOR USING THIS EXERCISE WITH FAMILIES

Peer group values and expectations can influence children of all ages, especially those between the ages of 8 and 16. This activity directs the parents and the child to identify peer pressures and to compare and contrast their opinions as to the effects the peer group is having upon the child's behavior, attitude, and decisionmaking. The parents are encouraged to initiate discussions regarding peer values versus family values before the child reaches the critical ages of being influenced primarily by peer behavior, and to continue the conversation until the child reaches adulthood. The ongoing identification of peer expectations will keep the parents informed and involved and help the child make positive decisions about life-altering issues.

PEER PRESSURES, VALUES, AND INFLUENCES

INSTRUCTIONS FOR THE PARENTS AND THE CHILD

Peers group fashions, ideas, and expectations affect people of all ages, but are probably strongest upon children between the ages of 8 to 16. Children eight and under typically view their parents as their primary source of guidance, while young adults 16 and over are beginning to rely more upon their own opinions and values. However, peer expectations remain important throughout one's lifetime, and their influence should be acknowledged as a persuasive element in every person's decisionmaking process.

The parents' and the child's estimation of how the peer group influences opinions, values, behavior, and decisionmaking may vary slightly or substantially. It is helpful to discuss the power of the peer group and to determine if this power is having a positive, neutral, or negative effect upon the child. Although it is impossible to eliminate peer group pressure, by analyzing it's power and influence the parents and child can reduce the negative effects upon the child's critical areas of functioning.

Create individual parent- and child-generated lists of the estimated influence the peer group is having upon the child's behavior, attitude, and decisionmaking. Discuss areas where the two lists differ and where they are similar. Consider peer group values and pressure in the areas of clothes, achievement, extracurricular activities, friendships, music, tobacco, drugs and alcohol consumption, and sexual activity. Complete only the areas that are relevant to the peer group influence currently experienced by the child; add additional categories as appropriate.

Begin considering peer influences upon the child at the earliest possible age, and continue evaluating the effects as the child matures. Hold frequent discussions about the child's estimation of peer pressure as compared to the parent's perspective in all areas of the child's life. Initiating discussions about peer pressure in noncritical areas (e.g., clothes, music, extracurricular activities) will facilitate future discussions about the life-altering issues confronting the child (e.g., substance abuse, health-related habits, personal relationships, sexual activity, and goals for the future).

Clothes and Appearance

Child's Estimation of Peer Group Influence	Parents' Estimation of Peer Group Influence

Academic Achievement

Child's Estimation of Peer Group Influence	Parents' Estimation of Peer Group Influence

Extracurricular Activities

Child's Estimation of Peer Group Influence	Parents' Estimation of Peer Group Influence

Friendships

Child's Estimation of Peer Group Influence	Parents' Estimation of Peer Group Influence

Music

Child's Estimation of Peer Group Influence	Parents' Estimation of Peer Group Influence

Tobacco, Alcohol, and Drug Usage

Child's Estimation of Peer Group Influence	Parents' Estimation of Peer Group Influence

Sexual Activity

Child's Estimation of Peer Group Influence	Parents' Estimation of Peer Group Influence

Additional areas where peer group influence is experienced:

_____

Child's Estimation of Peer Group Influence	Parents' Estimation of Peer Group Influence

_____

Child's Estimation of Peer Group Influence	Parents' Estimation of Peer Group Influence

Child's Estimation of Peer Group Influence	Parents' Estimation of Peer Group Influence

Child's Estimation of Peer Group Influence	Parents' Estimation of Peer Group Influence

Child's Estimation of Peer Group Influence	Parents' Estimation of Peer Group Influence

POSTTRAUMATIC STRESS DISORDER (PTSD)

REFRAMING OUR WORRIES

GOALS OF THE EXERCISE

1. Verbalize an understanding of the reframing process.
2. Reframe situations that have triggered feelings of fear or anxiety.
3. Create encouraging and supportive self-talk to address stressful situations.
4. Identify the positive aspects of a challenging problem or situation.

ADDITIONAL HOMEWORK THAT MAY BE APPLICABLE TO POSTTRAUMATIC STRESS DISORDER

- Abusive Parenting   Measuring Our Feelings   Page 14
- Blended Family   Healing Hurt Feelings   Page 49
- Children with Physical Challenges   Working Together to Create a Plan   Page 102
- Divorce/Separation   Divorce is Not My Fault   Page 142

ADDITIONAL PROBLEMS THIS EXERCISE MAY BE MOST USEFUL FOR

- Abusive Parenting
- Blended Family
- Depression
- Divorce
- Grief/Loss

SUGGESTIONS FOR USING THIS EXERCISE WITH FAMILIES

This activity is based on the Rational Emotive techniques outlined in *A New Guide to Rational Living* by Ellis (Wilshire Book Co., 1978). Families experiencing a high level of anxiety and destabilizing traumatic events tend to "awfulize" and "catastrophize" their problems; their self-talk becomes very negative and discouraging, and soon they see themselves as incapable of dealing with any challenging situation. The reframing process (e.g., reassessing a difficult situation from a different perspective that focuses on a more positive or solution-oriented approach) can help parents and children gain a sense of self-control and personal power.

REFRAMING OUR WORRIES

INSTRUCTIONS FOR THE PARENTS AND THE CHILD

Children and other family members who experience trauma related to serious disruption in their lives tend to be pessimistic about future scenarios that may occur. They tend to awfulize and catastrophize their assessment of daily situations rather than viewing past, current, and future events using a realistic and positive frame of reference. Defining a worst-case scenario and then reframing it to reflect a more optimistic and likely outcome can develop a healthier and more productive outlook. This process will help all family members strengthen their ability to cope with daily events and reduce the ongoing negative effects the trauma is having upon their lives.

Use the following reframing chart to record an ongoing list of worries experienced by you and your child, using an awfulizing/catastrophizing approach and then a realistic/positive perspective. This will help all family members recognize that a person's point of view greatly influences whether a problem is viewed as manageable and solvable or beyond human control.

After you have analyzed one or more initial problems, begin to apply this approach to several additional situations throughout the week. Use the activity sheet to record the process of moving from a helpless and hopeless to an empowered state of mind. Discuss each recorded scenario with your family counselor or during a family meeting.

Examples:

Situation	Awfulizing/Catastrophizing	Realistic/Positive
I lost my boyfriend.	There is nothing I can do. I cry all the time. I can't focus on my studies. I'll never find another true love. I have to get him back. He thinks I'm a loser. All my friends will drop me. He's my whole life. I have no reason to live.	I am lonely but I am young and fun. I have other friends. It will be hard but I can get through this. There are plenty of other boys. I wasn't ready to get serious anyway. Perhaps he wasn't the right one for me.
Dad cancelled our Wednesday evening visit.	Dad never wants to see me. He'd much rather be with his other family. I'll probably never hear from him again. I know he doesn't really love me.	Dad has another important appointment. He said he wants to reschedule with me and I should choose the time. He told me he really loves me and wants to see me. I'll call him and arrange another get-together.

REFRAMING OUR WORRIES

Record several of your prominent worries, using a worst-case scenario and an optimistic, solution-oriented approach for each. Try to think of as many positive ways to consider the problem as possible.

Situation	Awfulizing/Catastrophizing	Realistic/Positive

PHYSICAL RECEPTORS OF STRESS

GOALS OF THE EXERCISE

1. Identify how stress is demonstrated in physical symptoms.
2. Recognize the positive and negative effects of stress.
3. Differentiate between long- and short-term stress.
4. Implement techniques to counter the negative effects of chronic stress.

ADDITIONAL HOMEWORK THAT MAY BE APPLICABLE TO POSTTRAUMATIC STRESS REDUCTION

• Eating Disorder	Modeling Healthy Attitudes about Nutrition, Exercise, and Body Image	Page 156
• Grief/Loss	Monitoring Our Reactions to Change and Loss	Page 184
• Peer Relationships/Influences	Peer Pressures, Values, and Influences	Page 207
• Prenatal Parenting Preparation	Creating a Family-Friendly Lifestyle	Page 238

ADDITIONAL PROBLEMS THIS EXERCISE MAY BE MOST USEFUL FOR

- Eating Disorder
- Attention-Deficit/Hyperactivity Disorder (ADHD)
- Depression
- Divorce
- Grief/Loss
- Prenatal Parenting Preparation

SUGGESTIONS FOR USING THIS EXERCISE WITH FAMILIES

The Physical Receptors of Stress activity helps the parents and the child to pinpoint the areas in their bodies that harbor anxiety and stress. The parents are directed to review the short- and long-term results of stress with the child and to consider the positive and negative effects upon physical, mental, and emotional functioning. Short-term stress is defined as helpful for coping with daily and unique challenges, whereas long-term stress is defined as harmful and debilitating. The family is directed to engage in stress reducing activities to combat the negative effects of long-term stress and to discuss the results with their family counselor or during a family meeting.

PHYSICAL RECEPTORS OF STRESS

INSTRUCTIONS FOR THE PARENTS AND THE CHILD

Stress is created by the body's natural reaction to a perceived threat or problem and the resulting fight-or-flight response (intended originally for self-protection). Stress reactors were designed to deal with a problem within a short period of time and then return to a more normal and relaxed state. Chronic or constant stress keeps the body's alert systems active over long periods of time. This causes both physical and mental damage as a result of the toxic chemicals (adrenaline and cortisol) that remain in the system, rather than being released from the body as nature intended. Constant stress can lead to a diminished cognitive ability, fatigue, anger, depression, suppression of the immune system, and many other physical and emotional problems. Symptoms of chronic stress can often be harbored in particular parts of the body and are indicated by tightness, stiffness, weakness, or pain (e.g., tight jaw, headache, shoulder or neck pain, stomach ache, lower back pain, chest pains).

Assign family members to track where stress affects their body most often by individually completing the activity on the next page. Use a pencil or colored marker to pinpoint the areas where stress is experienced during the following week. Each time the parents or the child feel a physical reaction to stress, record the location on the activity sheet. This process will help to identify how the body reacts to challenging situations.

Some antidotes for the physical and emotional symptoms of stress include: listening to music, aerobic exercise, sequential muscle relaxation, rhythmical breathing, humor, relaxation tapes, talking with a friend, and so on. Talk with your family counselor about how these antidotes can help family members to deal with daily and unique challenges without becoming overly stressed or developing physical symptoms. Encourage each family member to choose one of the antidotes and practice it during the week. Report the results of the family's stress-fighting program during your next counseling session or during a family meeting.

PHYSICAL RECEPTORS OF STRESS

Long- and Short-Term Effects of Stress

Paste or draw an outline of a human figure similar to yourself in the box. Record the most common areas where you feel stress in your body during the following week.

Short-term stress makes us more mentally and physically alert and able to deal with problems.

Long-term or chronic stress threatens our physical and mental health.

Short-term results:

The body prepares to deal with a problem.

Long-term results:

The body is unable to release harmful chemicals designed to cope with short-term stress.

- **Brain:** Improved thinking and reduced sense of pain.

- **Eyes:** Improved vision.

- **Lungs:** Increased oxygen intake.

- **Heart:** Increased heart rate and blood pressure.

- **Adrenal glands:** Adrenaline released into body.

- **Intestines:** Digestion stops to allow for increased energy in muscles.

- **Hair:** Body hairs stand up.

- **Brain:** Released Cortisol becomes harmful to brain cells. Fatigue, anger, and depression result.

- **Immune system:** Weakened resistance to disease.

- **Intestines:** Reduction of blood flow increases chance of ulcers.

- **Circulation:** Higher blood pressure and heart rate. Damaged blood vessels.

Section XX

POVERTY-RELATED ISSUES

ACHIEVING FAMILY GOALS

GOALS OF THE EXERCISE

1. Recognize that planning is necessary for goal achievement.
2. Identify the family's long- and short-term goals.
3. Recognize resources available to assist the family in goal attainment.
4. Develop and commit to a plan for goal achievement.

ADDITIONAL HOMEWORK THAT MAY BE APPLICABLE TO GOAL ACHIEVEMENT

- Oppositional Defiant Disorder (ODD) Family-Approved Media List Page 198
- School Adjustment Difficulties Organizing for the School Day Page 248
- Strategies for Children (Ages 7 to 12) Problem-solving Worksheet Page 323
- Strategies for Preschoolers (Ages Birth to 6) Helping My Child Develop Responsible Behavior Page 305

ADDITIONAL PROBLEMS THIS EXERCISE MAY BE MOST USEFUL FOR

- Oppositional Defiant Behavior
- School Adjustment Difficulties
- Strategies for Preschoolers (Ages Birth to 6)
- Strategies for Children (Ages 7 to 12)
- Strategies for Teenagers (Ages 13 to 18)

SUGGESTIONS FOR USING THIS EXERCISE WITH FAMILIES

This activity will help the family define a specific goal, identify the resources available to help attain the goal, as well as identify the potential roadblocks to success. Family members are then instructed to list the steps required to reach the goal, commit to making a united effort and, finally, sign and date the plan. The worksheet can be used repeatedly as the family prepares to work toward specific short- and long-term goals. The plans can be kept in a family journal and reviewed at a family meeting to help members recognize the key elements of a successful plan and revise plans that are not working. The process of planing and organizing for goal attainment is a skill that will be useful to all family members throughout their lifetimes.

ACHIEVING FAMILY GOALS

INSTRUCTIONS FOR THE PARENTS AND THE CHILD

All goal achievement takes planning—whether it's a national goal, like putting a man on the moon, or a family goal, like helping a child get better grades in school. There are important steps to successful goal achievement for both large and small family goals. It is helpful to identify the goal and then describe specific plans for achieving it. The steps involved in reaching a family goal are:

1. Identify the goal.

2. List the resources or the help and support available to help achieve the family goal.

3. List any challenges or roadblocks that may interfere with reaching the goal.

4. Create a plan for achieving the goal by listing the steps necessary for success.

5. Write a statement that commits family members to working toward the goal.

Following is an example of a goal achievement plan developed by a third grade student and his parents.

Family Goal: To help Jason improve his math grade from a C to a B during the next six weeks' grading period.

List some resources available to help you to achieve the goal.

- Jason's teacher said she would help him in class or during recess.

- Uncle Charley is good at math and he could tutor Jason at home.

- Jason is really committed to improving his math grade.

- Mom and Dad support and encourage Jason to improve his math grade.

List some roadblocks or challenges in achieving this goal.

- Math is hard for Jason.

- Jason would rather go out for recess than stay in and study with his teacher.

- It's noisy at home after supper and the TV makes it hard for Jason to concentrate.

- Jason's uncle isn't always home to help him.

- Sometimes Jason has difficulty concentrating during math class.

Create a strategy and list the steps involved in achieving your family goal.

1. Jason agrees to try really hard to concentrate during math class.

2. Dad will ask Uncle Charley which nights he can be home to help Jason with his math.

3. Jason agrees to do his homework at the kitchen table where he can't see the TV, and use earplugs, if necessary, to keep out the noise.

4. Mom and Dad agree to keep the TV and other household noise to a bare minimum during study time.

5. Jason will ask his teacher to help him during class so he won't have to stay in for recess.

6. Jason agrees to correct all of his mistakes on his math papers and to ask his teacher to check his work.

7. Jason and his parents will keep track of all his math grades to make sure he is doing B or better work.

8. Jason and his parents will share their plan with his teacher and ask if she has any other suggestions.

Write your commitment to achieving your goal.

We will work together as a family to support Jason and his efforts to improve his grades in math from a C to a B or better. Jason will give math his best effort and will participate fully in the family's plan to improve his math performance. If we find that this plan isn't working, we will talk with Jason's teacher and work together with Jason to develop a better plan for success.

Now, develop a plan for achievement of a family goal.

Goal Achievement

Define the family goal. _____

_____

List some resources available to assist in achieving the goal.

_____

_____

_____

List some roadblocks or challenges in achieving this goal.

_____

_____

_____

Create a strategy and list the steps involved in achieving this goal.

1. _____

2. _____

3. _____

4. _____

5. _____

6. _____

7. _____

8. _____

Write your commitment to achieving the goal.

_____

_____

_____

Signed: _____   _____

_____   _____

_____   _____

Date: _____

DIFFERENT RULES FOR HOME AND SCHOOL

GOALS OF THE EXERCISE

1. Recognize that various settings and circumstances have different standards for behavior.
2. Identify specific rules that apply at school and at home.
3. Demonstrate the ability to adjust to different standards for behavior in various settings.
4. Cooperate with school and classroom rules and discipline structure.

ADDITIONAL HOMEWORK THAT MAY BE APPLICABLE TO COOPERATION WITH SCHOOL AND FAMILY RULES

• Career Preparation	Career Family Tree	Page 72
	School-to-Career Diary	Page 78
• Character Development	Division of Family Labor	Page 86
• Divorce/Separation	Assuming Our Parental Responsibilities	Page 145
• Grandparenting Strategies	Parents' Rules versus Grandparents' Rules	Page 172

ADDITIONAL PROBLEMS THIS EXERCISE MAY BE MOST USEFUL FOR

- Career Preparation
- Character Development
- Divorce/Separation
- Grandparenting Strategies
- School Adjustment Difficulties

SUGGESTIONS FOR USING THIS EXERCISE WITH FAMILIES

Children come to school from various backgrounds and their families may have rules and systems of discipline that are quite different from the school rules and discipline structure. The *Different Rules for Home and School* activity helps the family define the similarities and differences between limits that are set at home and those that are set at school. Recognition that there are various standards for behavior established for specific settings and circumstances will help the child and parents adjust to the separate requirements of school and home.

DIFFERENT RULES FOR HOME AND SCHOOL

INSTRUCTIONS FOR THE PARENTS AND THE CHILD

Often the rules at home and the rules at school are different. For example, at home the child can probably watch TV and eat at the same time; however, at school, eating must be done in the lunchroom or on special occasions in the classroom. Perhaps there are different rules for the way the child speaks to the teacher and the parents, for where to put belongings, for when to work and when to play, and so on. Most people live with, and follow, two or more sets of rules. There are different rules for home, school, work, church, movie theaters, sports events, and restaurants. Understanding and learning to follow different rules for different situations helps all family members to be appropriate and successful in all of their experiences and activities. Following are some situations where the rules at home may differ from the rules at school. Work together to write the school rule first, and then write the rule for home.

Rules At School   **Rules At Home**

Speaking to an adult

_____   _____

_____   _____

Fighting

_____   _____

_____   _____

Where food is eaten

_____   _____

_____   _____

Doing chores or schoolwork

_____   _____

_____   _____

Speaking to your siblings or classmates

_____   _____

_____   _____

Attitude and behavior when being disciplined

_____   _____

_____   _____

Sarcasm and put-downs

_____   _____

_____   _____

Taking care of belongings

_____   _____

_____   _____

Borrowing from others

_____   _____

_____   _____

Interrupting others

_____   _____

_____   _____

Sharing

_____   _____

_____   _____

Consequences for inappropriate behavior

_____   _____

_____   _____

Acceptable use of language

_____   _____

_____   _____

Table manners

_____   _____

_____   _____

Playground or outdoor behavior

_____   _____

_____   _____

Time for work and play

_____   _____

_____   _____

Who makes and enforces the rules

_____   _____

_____   _____

Section XXI

PRENATAL PARENTING PREPARATION

CREATING A FAMILY-FRIENDLY LIFESTYLE

GOALS OF THE EXERCISE

1. Identify habits that contribute to a healthy pregnancy and birth.
2. Identify characteristics and behaviors that threaten a healthy pregnancy and birth.
3. Determine unhealthy habits that need to be replaced with healthy habits.
4. Parents agree to adopt a family-friendly lifestyle prior to the pregnancy and birth.

ADDITIONAL HOMEWORK THAT MAY BE APPLICABLE TO PRENATAL PARENTING PREPARATION

• Single Parenting	Stress Reduction Strategies	Page 276
• Spousal Role and Relationship Conflict	State of Our Marriage Report	Page 282
• Eating Disorder	Modeling Healthy Attitudes about Nutrition, Exercise, and Body Image	Page 156
• Substance Abuse	Our Commitment to a Substance-Free Lifestyle	Page 348

ADDITIONAL PROBLEMS THIS EXERCISE MAY BE MOST USEFUL FOR

- Single Parenting
- Poverty-related Issues
- Spousal Role and Relationship Conflict
- Strategies for Teenagers

SUGGESTIONS FOR USING THIS EXERCISE WITH FAMILIES

An essential part of prenatal parenting preparation is to review the couple's existing lifestyle and analyze current habits that will contribute to or threaten successful parenthood. This activity provides a list of family-friendly characteristics and a list of unhealthy habits, and directs the prospective parents to record additional behaviors and traits from their own lifestyle. The couple determines which unhealthy behaviors should be modified and commits to replace their unproductive habits with healthy habits, in order to prepare for a successful pregnancy and effective parenting of their newborn.

CREATING A FAMILY-FRIENDLY LIFESTYLE

INSTRUCTIONS FOR THE EXPECTANT PARENTS

Prospective parents have developed a lifestyle that meets their needs as individuals or a couple without children, and the introduction of a pregnancy and the birth of an infant into their world will radically change their environment and lifestyle forever. Some existing habits may be very compatible with parenthood, while other routines and behaviors will cause distress for the pregnant couple and their baby. Below is a list of healthy and unhealthy habits that young adults sometimes engage in. Look over the lists and add those current behaviors that will prepare you for successful parenthood and those that will be problematic once you become pregnant. Choose two or three of the habits that will need to be eliminated or modified, and work together to create a plan for a more family-friendly lifestyle.

Family Friendly Habits and Traits	Unhealthy Habits for Prospective Parents
Exercise regularly	Alcohol and drug usage
Eat a healthy diet	Binge or unhealthy eating
A positive relationship with the extended family	Difficulty resolving problems with spouse
Take problems in stride	Excessive or low level of energy
Avoid alcohol and drugs	Lack of or excessive exercise
A moderate to high level of energy	Lack of organization
Talk out problems as a couple	Lack of personal and household hygiene
Balance family life and work	Narcissistic personality
Enjoy and am comfortable with children	Perfectionist personality
Enjoy spending time at home	Poor relationship with prospective co-parent

Family Friendly Habits and Traits	Unhealthy Habits for Prospective Parents
Have a supportive circle of friends	Poor relationship with the extended family
Compassion for others	Resistant to becoming a parent
Manage my time wisely	Sleep-deprived
Get plenty of rest	Smoking
Maintain clean and safe living arrangements	Social isolation
Manage my anger appropriately	Uncomfortable around children
Exercise moderately several times per week	Uncontrolled anger and/or abuse
Avoid smoking and smoky rooms	Work long hours

To better prepare for a successful pregnancy and a healthy, happy new baby in our lives we will need to eliminate or modify several of our existing behaviors and replace them with the family-friendly behaviors that follow:

Unhealthy Habits for Prospective Parents	Family Friendly Habits and Traits

Now create a plan for replacing unhealthy habits with family-friendly habits.

Example:

Our plan for eliminating lack of exercise and having no time to talk with one another (unhealthy habits) is to take a walk each evening and talk about our plans to start a family and develop a more family-friendly lifestyle.

Our plan for eliminating _____ (unhealthy habit) is to _____

_____

_____

_____

_____

Our plan for eliminating _____ (unhealthy habit) is to _____

_____

_____

_____

_____

We agree to work together to create a more family-friendly lifestyle, so that our new baby can experience parents who are prepared to offer lifelong love, compassion, guidance, support, and encouragement.

_____   _____

Date: _____

BONDING WITH OUR PRENATAL BABY

GOALS OF THE EXERCISE

1. Create a loving bond between the expectant parents and the prenatal infant.
2. Identify strategies for both parents to express love and caring to the prenatal baby.
3. Encourage participation of both parents in the care and nurturing of the unborn infant.
4. Record prenatal care and bonding activities in a baby journal for future reference.

ADDITIONAL HOMEWORK THAT MAY BE APPLICABLE TO PRENATAL PARENTING PREPARATION

• Single Parenting	Stress Reduction Strategies	Page 276
• Spousal Role and Relationship Conflict	Our Evolving Marriage and Spousal Roles	Page 287
• Strategies for Teenagers (Ages 13 to 18)	Listening with Empathy	Page 330
• Substance Abuse	Our Commitment to a Substance-Free Lifestyle	Page 348

ADDITIONAL PROBLEMS THIS EXERCISE MAY BE MOST USEFUL FOR

- Single Parenting
- Poverty-related Issues
- Spousal Role and Relationship Conflict
- Strategies for Teenagers

SUGGESTIONS FOR USING THIS EXERCISE WITH FAMILIES

The essential bonding process between the prenatal baby and parents begins from the moment the couple becomes aware of the pregnancy. The desire to protect, love, and nurture the baby is an extension of the attachment the parents feel toward their unborn child. This activity helps parents to develop an awareness of the prenatal care requirements and interactions that promote a loving bond between themselves and their baby. A record is kept of all parental activities that encourage bonding and of the response of the prenatal baby and the parents. This ongoing record will encourage and reinforce the parents' efforts to communicate with their unborn infant, and can be referred to later as a loving reminder to the child of the parents' caring gestures and involvement from the earliest stages of pregnancy.

BONDING WITH OUR PRENATAL BABY

INSTRUCTIONS FOR THE EXPECTANT PARENTS

Feelings of attachment to the prenatal baby begin very early in the pregnancy, and increase as the baby grows and develops. Feelings of love and excitement begin for both parents, usually right after the pregnancy has been confirmed. The parent/child bond intensifies as the baby begins to make physical demands upon the mother; she can feel movement, and her body begins to grow and change with the development of the fetus. The father can observe and become intimately involved with these changes as he begins to attach to the baby through his relationship with the mother and his own emotions of warmth, love, and pride. Both parents can encourage and intensify the creation of a loving bond with their baby by engaging in interactive activities that generate a sense of love and caring, and begin to establish the preliminary communication so important to the close relationship they will develop with their child, both before and after birth.

Many activities recommended by healthcare providers to ensure the development of a healthy prenatal baby (e.g., regular prenatal check ups, proper nutrition, elimination of unhealthy substances and activities from the parents' lifestyles, moderate exercise) also contribute to the feelings of love and attachment that evolve in the parents. This is nature's way of ensuring that the baby is protected and cared for by nurturing and loving parents. Additional and optional activities can create an even stronger invisible bond of love between the unborn infant and the parents (e.g., singing to the baby, dancing with the baby, reading to the baby, lightly massaging the baby). A strong attachment between the infant and parents is the essential basis for the future healthy development of the child—physically, mentally, and emotionally. The critical nature of this bond cannot be overestimated.

Begin a list of all the activities that can contribute to a stronger loving bond with the baby. Be creative in discovering new ways to communicate with your developing infant. Record the parental responses that you are experiencing and any responses that are generated from the prenatal baby (e.g., movement, gurgling, hiccups, peacefulness). Continue to document as much prenatal baby/parent interaction as possible and save the information in the baby's book or journal. This information will be fun, interesting, and affirming, when shared with the child later, as another way of expressing parental love and attachment.

Examples:

Bonding Activity	Date	Baby's Response	Parents' Response
First prenatal checkup	July 22	Identity established	Excitement, joy, love, fear
Ultrasound	Oct. 22	Movement	Love, joy, amazement
Singing to baby	Nightly	Gurgled	Peaceful, restful
Dancing with baby	Nov.–March	Restful	Enjoyed the movement
Feeling the baby kicking	Nov. 20	Kicked harder	Laughing, communicating with one another about the baby

Bonding With Our Prenatal Baby

Bonding Activity	Date	Baby's Response	Parents' Response

Bonding Activity	Date	Baby's Response	Parents' Response

SCHOOL ADJUSTMENT DIFFICULTIES

ORGANIZING FOR THE SCHOOL DAY

GOALS OF THE EXERCISE

1. Organize for the school day.
2. List materials necessary for daily school success.
3. Record forgotten items on the materials checklist.
4. Develop the child's planning and organizational skills.

ADDITIONAL HOMEWORK THAT MAY BE APPLICABLE TO PLANNING FOR THE SCHOOL DAY

- Attention-Deficit/ Hyperactivity Disorder (ADHD)

  Family Problem Resolution Worksheet   Page 29

- Posttraumatic Stress Disorder (PTSD)

  Reframing Our Worries   Page 216
  Physical Receptors of Stress   Page 220

- Single Parenting

  Stress Reduction Strategies   Page 276

ADDITIONAL PROBLEMS THIS EXERCISE MAY BE MOST USEFUL FOR

- Attention-Deficit/Hyperactivity Disorder (ADHD)
- Grief/Loss
- Posttraumatic Stress Disorder (PTSD)
- Single Parenting

SUGGESTIONS FOR USING THIS EXERCISE WITH FAMILIES

Feeling unprepared for school can contribute to a child's anxiety and to phobic feelings about going to school. This activity directs the parents and child to prepare for the school day, by organizing all of the materials that will be needed and by selecting from a provided list of examples and adding additional items as needed. The parents are advised to oversee the child's organization of all necessary items at night before bed, and re-check the child's school bag or backpack in the morning to make sure everything has been included. The process puts the child in charge of preparing for school and helps to develop self-reliance, organizational skills, and a feeling of empowerment that will reduce feelings of insecurity about school attendance.

ORGANIZING FOR THE SCHOOL DAY

INSTRUCTIONS FOR THE PARENTS AND THE CHILD

Part of feeling confident about one's child attending school is making sure he or she will have all the materials necessary to be successful in school that day. The process of getting organized makes participating in any activity much easier. It is helpful to think about the school day in small segments, and to have the child list what is needed for each class or hour of the day. Start by listing all the classes and activities and the materials required for each. Some essentials for school success are listed below, but it is important to add to the list to make it fit the child's unique situation in his or her particular classes and school.

assignments	crayons	musical instrument
backpack	eraser	notebooks
bike	games or toys	paper
bike lock	gloves	pencils
books	gym clothes	permission slips
boots	gym shoes	planner
class project	homework	snack
coat	lunch	sports equipment
computer disks	lunch money	sweater

Add some materials necessary for a successful school day.

_____   _____   _____

_____   _____   _____

_____   _____   _____

_____   _____   _____

_____   _____   _____

Now, help the child determine what materials will be needed for each school day during the following week.

Before-school Activities:

Example: Riding the bus

_____

_____

_____

Materials I Will Need:

Games or toys

_____

_____

_____

First Hour Activities:

Example: Teacher takes lunch count

_____

_____

_____

Materials I Will Need:

Lunch money or packed lunch

_____

_____

_____

Second Hour Activities:

Example: Language Arts

_____

_____

_____

Materials I Will Need:

Homework, paper, pencils

_____

_____

_____

Third Hour Activities:

Example: Physical Education

_____

_____

_____

Materials I Will Need:

Gym clothes and shoes

_____

_____

_____

Lunch Hour Activities:

Example: Eat lunch

_____

_____

_____

Materials I Will Need:

Lunch money or packed lunch

_____

_____

_____

After Lunch First Hour Activities:

Example: Computer class

_____

_____

_____

Materials I Will Need:

Computer disk and book

_____

_____

_____

After Lunch Second Hour Activities:

Example: Music class

_____

_____

_____

Materials I Will Need:

Musical instrument

_____

_____

_____

Third Hour Activities:

Example: Math class

_____

_____

_____

Materials I Will Need:

Homework, book, pencils, paper

_____

_____

_____

Preparing To Go Home:

Example: Bus ride home

_____

_____

_____

Materials I Will Need:

Assignments, books, backpack, coat

_____

_____

_____

Assist the child to create a personal list and to organize all necessary materials for school the night before. In the morning, encourage the child to double-check the school bag or backpack. This process will help the child to feel prepared and confident about going to school. Advise the child to take the list to school and to add any forgotten item so it will be remembered the next day. Gradually the child will become more and more organized, and this will add to the overall enjoyment of school and related activities.

MY IDEAL SCHOOL DAY

GOALS OF THE EXERCISE

1. Design the ideal school day.
2. The parents and the child visualize the child as successfully participating in school.
3. Compare an actual school day with an idealized school day.
4. Identify strategies for improving the school experience.

ADDITIONAL HOMEWORK THAT MAY BE APPLICABLE TO IMPROVING SCHOOL ATTENDANCE

• Career Preparation	School-to-Career Diary	Page 78
• Children with Physical Challenges	Strategies for Supporting Our Child with Physical Challenges	Page 100
• Posttraumatic Stress Disorder (PTSD)	Reframing Our Worries	Page 216
• Poverty-related Issues	Different Rules for Home and School	Page 231

ADDITIONAL PROBLEMS THIS EXERCISE MAY BE MOST USEFUL FOR

- Career Preparation
- Children with Physical Challenges
- Posttraumatic Stress Disorder (PTSD)
- Poverty-related Issues

SUGGESTIONS FOR USING THIS EXERCISE WITH FAMILIES

Designing the perfect school day can help the family picture the child as successfully participating in the school curriculum. This activity instructs the parents and child to imagine a perfect school day and then to write a story involving the idealized experience. Sentence starters are provided to help the family organize and construct the story. The parents and child are then asked to write another short story describing a typical school day. Finally, the parents assist the child to compare and contrast the two stories and to determine how aspects of the ideal school day could be incorporated into an actual school day. Six follow-up questions focus on the similarities and differences between the two days, and on strategies that the parents and child can implement to produce an improved reality at school.

MY IDEAL SCHOOL DAY

INSTRUCTIONS FOR THE PARENTS AND THE CHILD

Work together as parents and child to discuss and envision the perfect school day. What would this day look, sound, smell, and feel like to the child? Describe this school day from the early morning routine to the return home from school. How will the child wake up? What will the child eat for breakfast? What are ideal school clothes? How will the child get to school? How do the teacher and other students greet the child? Use some of the sentence starters below to write a story about the perfect school day from the child's perspective. Try to include as many positive and productive ideas as possible, as this will help to positively influence the actual school experience. After you have collaborated on a story about the perfect school day, work together to write a story describing an actual or typical school day, and compare and contrast the two scenarios by helping the child to answer the follow-up questions.

I wake up at … (time)

When … (what or who wakes you up)

The first person I see is …

Who says …

For breakfast I have …

My breakfast is fixed for me by …

I get dressed and put on …

I get to school using my favorite transportation, which is …

When I get to school the first thing I do is …

The first person in school I see is …

Who says …

When I get to my classroom my teacher says …

We begin my favorite activity, which is …

The next thing I do is …

Other things we do in the morning are …

I eat my favorite lunch, which is …

During lunch …

After lunch …

During recess …

After recess …

Other things we do in the afternoon are …

I get to work with …

My favorite activity today was …

On the way home …

After my perfect day I want to …

I hope that tomorrow …

My Perfect Day in School

_____

_____

_____

_____

_____

_____

_____

_____

_____

_____

A Typical Day in School

_____

_____

_____

_____

_____

_____

_____

_____

_____

_____

Now compare the perfect school day with a typical school day.

The major difference between a perfect school day and a typical school day is:

_____

_____

The first thing about the typical school day I would like to change is:

_____

_____

Some things in my ideal school day that happen in a typical school day are:

_____

_____

Some things about the typical school day that I would like to remain are:

_____

_____

Something I could do to make my ideal school day more real is to:

_____

_____

Another thing I could do to make my ideal school day more real is to:

_____

_____

Section XXIII

SEXUAL RESPONSIBILITY

SEXUAL RESPONSIBILITY AND HEALTHY SELF-ESTEEM

GOALS OF THE EXERCISE

1. Encourage the child to gain a sense of control over positive and negative relationships.
2. Recognize the symptoms of healthy and unhealthy relationships.
3. Identify the connection between relationships and self-esteem.
4. Assist the child to learn assertive responses to put-downs and harassment.

ADDITIONAL HOMEWORK THAT MAY BE APPLICABLE TO SEXUAL RESPONSIBILITY

• Depression	Creating Positive Self-Talk	Page 130
	Managing Positive and Negative Relationships	Page 134
• School Adjustment Difficulties	My Ideal School Day	Page 252
• Suicide Prevention	Heart-to-Heart Smart Talks	Page 354

ADDITIONAL PROBLEMS THIS EXERCISE MAY BE MOST USEFUL FOR

- Depression
- School Adjustment Difficulties
- Suicide Prevention
- Strategies for Teenagers (Ages 13 to 18)
- Substance Abuse

SUGGESTIONS FOR USING THIS EXERCISE WITH FAMILIES

This activity defines for parents and child the attributes of a healthy and unhealthy relationship, and the effects of each upon self-esteem. Unhealthy relationships are characterized as contributing to feelings of discouragement, disrespect, self-doubt, and low self-esteem, whereas positive relationships are described as supportive, caring, and encouraging to healthy self-esteem. The child, with the assistance of his or her parents, is instructed to list several important personal relationships and describe the characteristics of each. They are then guided to evaluate each relationship as having a positive or negative effect upon the child's emotional health. Suggestions for dealing with negative relationships are provided, and the child is directed to choose one or more strategy to respond to disrespectful actions or harassment.

SEXUAL RESPONSIBILITY AND HEALTHY SELF-ESTEEM

INSTRUCTIONS FOR THE PARENTS AND THE CHILD

The child or adolescent should complete the following activity with the assistance of the parents. Discuss each concept using communication strategies that promote an open, nonjudgmental exchange of ideas (e.g., "I"-statements, reflective listening). The parents are encouraged to allow the child to take the lead in answering the questions and to offer input and guidance as needed.

Children and adolescents with healthy self-esteem usually choose healthy relationships; conversely, those with low self-esteem choose unhealthy relationships that further reduce their level of self-respect. One of the best ways to enhance healthy self-esteem is to choose friendships and relationships that support personal strengths, encourage success, and promote a sense of empowerment. If you are associated with friends that focus on your weaknesses and contribute to feelings of insecurity, helplessness, and hopelessness, it may be time to reevaluate why you allow these relationships to be part of your life. Two lists of words follow: the first describes healthy relationships, the second, unhealthy or abusive relationships.

Healthy Relationships Involve:

Accountability	Independence
Caring	Individuality
Communication	Mutual respect
Compromise	Openness
Empathy	Shared responsibility
Equality	Support
Ethics	Trust
Fairness	Win/Win Results
Honesty	

Unhealthy Relationships Involve:

Blame	Perpetrators
Control	Put-downs
Dishonesty	Sexism
Fear	Submission
Guilt	Sulking
Harassment	Victims
Insecurity	Win/Lose Results
Jealousy	Withdrawal
Manipulation	

Name six of the most important friendships in your life and list the descriptors that characterize your relationship with each person.

Name: Characteristics:

1. _____   _____

2. _____   _____

3. _____   _____

4. _____   _____

5. _____   _____

6. _____   _____

Which of your relationships are supporting healthy self-esteem and feelings of empowerment?

_____

_____

Which of your relationships are contributing to low self-esteem and feelings of discouragement?

_____

_____

How do you plan to deal with the relationships that are destructive to your emotional well-being?

_____

_____

How do you plan to deal with the positive relationships in your life?

_____

_____

One way to handle destructive relationships, which tear down your self-esteem, is to respond to criticism, put-downs, and harassing remarks with assertive statements. Some ways to respond to disrespectful comments are:

"I"-statements:	"I feel extremely hurt when you speak to me that way."
It bugs me:	"It bugs me when you disrespect me that way; I wish you would stop."
Call it like it is:	"That's harassment; harassment is against the school policy."
Say what you will do:	"If this harassment continues, I will have to report it to the school administration."
Say something crazy:	"Purple Kumquat!"

Remember, you don't have to stay in an unhealthy, destructive relationship. You are able to choose your friends based upon mutual admiration and respect. The sooner you are able to establish positive friendships in your life the sooner you will begin to admire and respect yourself and begin to build healthy self-esteem. Harassment and putdowns are common in unhealthy relationships. When someone tries to put you down by making a negative remark use one of the preceding responses and move away from that person. Hang out with positive people and you will find that you become much happier and more positive yourself.

The next time someone is disrespectful to me I will say:

_____

or

_____

If that doesn't work I will:

_____

or

_____

MY PERSONAL SEXUAL RESPONSIBILITY CODE

GOALS OF THE EXERCISE

1. Encourage the child to commit to ethical sexual behavior.
2. Assist the child to seek sexual information from knowledgeable and responsible sources.
3. Define sexual integrity.
4. Encourage the child to make positive choices concerning sexual behavior.

ADDITIONAL HOMEWORK THAT MAY BE APPLICABLE TO SEXUAL RESPONSIBILITY

• Attention-seeking Behavior	My Love and Trust Support Network	Page 42
• Conduct Disorder/Delinquent Behavior	Replacing Noncompliance with Compliance and Cooperation	Page 109
• Substance Abuse	Our Commitment to a Substance-Free Lifestyle	Page 348
• Suicide Prevention	Heart-to-Heart Smart Talks	Page 354

ADDITIONAL PROBLEMS THIS EXERCISE MAY BE MOST USEFUL FOR

- Responsible Behavior Training
- Character Development
- Conduct Disorder/Delinquent Behavior
- Strategies for Teenagers (Ages 13 to 18)
- Substance Abuse

SUGGESTIONS FOR USING THIS EXERCISE WITH FAMILIES

The "My Personal Sexual Responsibility Code" activity explores with the parents and child the meaning of sexual integrity and guides the child or adolescent to develop a personal standard for ethical sexual behavior. Adolescents often neglect to define their personal values, especially in the area of sexual responsibility. This leads to impulsive and reactive sexual behavior that is frequently detrimental to the child's physical and emotional health and jeopardizes future plans and aspirations. This activity defines the rationale for developing a sexual responsibility code and offers several examples of standards that adolescents typically choose as part of their commitment to healthy sexual behavior.

MY PERSONAL SEXUAL RESPONSIBILITY CODE

INSTRUCTIONS FOR THE PARENTS AND THE CHILD

The child or adolescent should complete the following activity with the assistance of the parents. Discuss each concept using communication strategies that promote an open, nonjudgmental exchange of ideas (e.g., "I"-statements, reflective listening). The parents are encouraged to allow the child to take the lead in developing a personal sexual responsibility code and to offer input and guidance as needed.

In order to treat oneself and others with regard, respect, and responsibility, it is important to develop a code of ethics or values that can guide personal decisions and behaviors. This is especially important in the area of sexual responsibility. Sexual integrity means acting with honesty, sincerity, and ethics when making choices that will affect oneself and others in the immediate future and for years to come. Consider some of the statements below, which are an example of values that other adolescents have incorporated into their personal sexual responsibility commitments. You may reword these statements and add additional values to define your own code of sexual behavior. Write your own personal sexual responsibility code to express your positive intentions in the area of ethical sexual behavior. When your code is complete, review it with your parents, sex education teacher, or your counselor, and revise your statements as needed. Finally indicate your commitment to sexual integrity by signing the code. Keep your code with you in a private place and review it frequently to insure that you use sexual responsibility when relating to others.

Statements Which Define Responsible Sexual Behavior:

- I will abstain from sexual intercourse until I am ready to begin my family.

- I will protect myself and others from the possibility of contracting an STD.

- I will protect myself and others from the possibility of getting pregnant.

- I will treat myself and others with respect when it comes to making sexual decisions.

- I will never try to force my sexual intentions upon others.

- I will take sexual education seriously, and attempt to learn as much about adolescent sexuality as possible from a credible source, such as school, religious, or community-sponsored classes.

- I will address my questions about sexuality to knowledgeable and respected adults (e.g., parents, teachers, counselors, doctors, religious advisors).

- I will not rush my sexual maturation process, and will relate to others in a friendly, age-appropriate manner, which will promote healthy relationships with friends of both sexes.

- I will seek medical advice whenever I have physical questions or concerns about my sexuality.

Add some responsible statements of your own for your personal responsibility code.

- _____
- _____
- _____
- _____
- _____
- _____

Now, write your personal code. When you have completed it and reviewed it with a responsible adult (e.g., parent, counselor, sexuality education teacher, religious advisor) sign it and keep it where you can read it and think about it often.

My Personal Sexual Responsibility Code

_____

_____

_____

_____

_____

_____

_____

_____

_____

_____

Signed: _____

Date: _____

Section XXIV

SIBLING RIVALRY

AFFIRMING EACH CHILD'S UNIQUENESS

GOALS OF THE EXERCISE

1. Affirm each child's unique characteristics and contributions to the family.
2. Reduce competition and rivalry among siblings.
3. Give unconditional love to each sibling.
4. Increase cooperation and harmony among all family members.

ADDITIONAL HOMEWORK THAT MAY BE APPLICABLE TO SIBLING RIVALRY

• Abusive Parenting	Measuring Our Feelings	Page 14
• Character Development	Sharing the Family Resources	Page 90
• Strategies for Children (Ages 7 to 12)	Record of Reinforced Behavior	Page 319
• Strategies for Preschoolers (Ages Birth to 6)	Charting Our Child's Developmental Stages	Page 298

ADDITIONAL PROBLEMS THIS EXERCISE MAY BE MOST USEFUL FOR

- Abusive Parenting
- Character Development
- School Adjustment Difficulties
- Strategies for Children (Ages 7 to 12)
- Substance Abuse

SUGGESTIONS FOR USING THIS EXERCISE WITH FAMILIES

Sibling rivalry is created when love, affirmations, and praise are awarded conditionally and unevenly among the siblings. This activity directs the parents to consider each child as special and unique and to offer frequent affirmations and unconditional love that nurtures a sense of security and healthy self-esteem. Positive affirmations, given frequently to each child, will develop a sense of cooperation among the siblings and reduce sibling rivalry which is often fueled by a competitive environment promoted by the parents. The parents are directed to list each child's unique positive characteristics and develop several affirmations to give the child during the following week. Affirming parents are very positive role models for their children, and teach the values of compassion, empathy, sharing, and teamwork. They teach their children to treat one another in the loving and affirming manner they have observed from their parents.

AFFIRMING EACH CHILD'S UNIQUENESS

INSTRUCTIONS FOR THE PARENTS

The birth of a new baby, or excessive competition among siblings of various ages, can create feelings of displacement, inadequacy, fears of loss of personal belongings and space, diminished parental love, reduced time with parents, loss of favored status in the family, and loss of personal control. Parents can help their children maintain or develop feelings of being safe, secure, and uniquely loved, by affirming each child's talents and abilities and by giving unconditional love to each child in the family. Sibling rivalry is fueled by parents who promote excessive competition among their children and share their love and admiration conditionally, sparingly, and unevenly, based on the comparative talents and behaviors of their children.

Frequent affirmations of each child's unique personality, talents, contributions, and behaviors can help to encourage a loving relationship among the siblings in the family. Affirmations build healthy self-esteem and feelings of self-assurance and security, which are essential ingredients for building sibling harmony and reducing sibling rivalry. Affirmations should be sincerely delivered, specific to the child being affirmed, and never a comparison to another sibling. Following is a list of affirmations that will promote positive feelings and encourage cooperation and support among the siblings. Review the list and add additional affirmations that are appropriate for the children in your family.

I love having you around.	You were so helpful with your brother tonight.
You like to meet new people.	You're so patient with your grandma.
I noticed that you smile while you're reading.	Nice job mowing the lawn.
You got dressed in five minutes.	You got an A on your science project!
I appreciate your help with washing the dishes.	You're a committed team player.
You picked up all of your toys!	Dad and I love watching you play basketball.
You're ready for bed in 10 minutes.	You're a loyal friend.

I love to hear you sing.	You unloaded all of the groceries—thanks!
Your hair has beautiful curls.	Your sister loves to play with you.
You're getting so strong!	You're a fast runner!

Choose three affirmations to deliver to each child in the family during the following week. Try to focus on the behaviors, abilities, and characteristics that are unique, admired, and support the goals and values of the child and the family. Help the children understand that your love and appreciation does not have to be competed for, because there is more than enough to go around.

Child's name: _____

Positive characteristics that should be affirmed:

_____   _____

_____   _____

_____   _____

_____   _____

Affirmations I plan to give my child during the following week:

_____

_____

_____

_____

Child's name: _____

Positive characteristics that should be affirmed:

_____   _____

_____   _____

_____   _____

_____   _____

Affirmations I plan to give my child during the following week:

_____

_____

_____

_____

Child's name: _____

Positive characteristics that should be affirmed:

_____   _____

_____   _____

_____   _____

_____   _____

Affirmations I plan to give my child during the following week:

_____

_____

_____

_____

Child's name: _____

Positive characteristics that should be affirmed:

_____   _____

_____   _____

_____   _____

_____   _____

Affirmations I plan to give my child during the following week:

_____

_____

_____

_____

Child's name: _____

Positive characteristics that should be affirmed:

_____   _____

_____   _____

_____   _____

_____   _____

Affirmations I plan to give my child during the following week:

_____

_____

_____

_____

SINGLE PARENTING

STRESS REDUCTION STRATEGIES

GOALS OF THE EXERCISE

1. Recognize the availability of many strategies to cope with anxiety.
2. Verbalize confidence in the ability to reduce personal anxiety.
3. Implement coping strategies to reduce symptoms of stress.
4. Recognize personal behavior that contributes to stress.

ADDITIONAL HOMEWORK THAT MAY BE APPLICABLE TO STRESS REDUCTION

- Posttraumatic Stress Disorder (PTSD)
  - Reframing Our Worries — Page 216
  - Physical Receptors of Stress — Page 220
- Grief/Loss
  - Monitoring Our Reactions to Change and Loss — Page 184
- School Adjustment Difficulties
  - Organizing for the School Day — Page 248

ADDITIONAL PROBLEMS THIS EXERCISE MAY BE MOST USEFUL FOR

- Divorce
- Grief/Loss
- Posttraumatic Stress Disorder (PTSD)
- School Adjustment Difficulties

SUGGESTIONS FOR USING THIS EXERCISE WITH PARENTS

This activity provides the single parent numerous strategies for dealing with stress. Often, an elevated level of anxiety is coupled with the perception that no viable solution for stress reduction exists. The parent is directed to indicate strategies that have already been tried and to select additional techniques for use during the following week. The effects of the interventions are recorded in a personal journal and reported to the counselor. Eventually, the parent is able to create a personalized list of effective stress reducers.

STRESS REDUCTION STRATEGIES

INSTRUCTIONS FOR THE SINGLE PARENT

Read over the following 101 stress reduction strategies and circle all of the strategies that you already use to cope with stress. Ask for an explanation of any of the ideas which are unclear or which you think may not work to reduce your level of stress. Determine which strategies are most helpful to you and choose one or two to use more frequently as stress-reducers during the following week. Discuss with your counselor why you have chosen these particular actions to reduce your level of stress.

During the next counseling session report to your counselor how the interventions you picked affected your level of stress during the week. Choose two additional strategies that you want to add to your stress reduction program. Continue to try different strategies to use during the weeks ahead and review the effects of each action during your next counseling session.

After several weeks of trying different methods of reducing your personal level of stress and anxiety, create your own top 10 list of effective stress reducers. Write this list in a personal journal and review and modify it occasionally throughout the year.

101 WAYS TO REDUCE STRESS

1. Get up earlier
2. Prepare ahead
3. Avoid tight clothes
4. Avoid chemical aids
5. Set appointments
6. Write it down
7. Practice preventive maintenance
8. Make duplicate keys
9. Say "no" more often
10. Set priorities
11. Avoid negative people
12. Use time wisely
13. Simplify meals
14. Copy important papers
15. Anticipate needs
16. Make repairs
17. Get help with jobs you dislike
18. Break down large tasks
19. Look at problems as challenges
20. Look at challenges differently
21. Unclutter your life
22. Smile

23. Prepare for rain

24. Tickle a baby

25. Pet a dog or cat

26. Don't know all the answers

27. Look for the silver lining

28. Say something nice

29. Teach a kid to fly a kite

30. Walk in the rain

31. Schedule play time

32. Take a bubble bath

33. Be aware of your decisions

34. Believe in yourself

35. Stop talking negatively

36. Visualize winning

37. Develop a sense of humor

38. Stop thinking tomorrow will be better

39. Have goals

40. Dance a jig

41. Say hello to a stranger

42. Ask a friend for a hug

43. Look at the stars

44. Breathe slowly

45. Whistle a tune

46. Read a poem

47. Listen to a symphony

48. Watch a ballet

49. Read a story

50. Do something new

51. Stop a bad habit

52. Buy a flower

53. Smell the flower

54. Find support

55. Find a "vent partner"

56. Do it today

57. Be optimistic

58. Put safety first

59. Do things in moderation

60. Note your appearance

61. Strive for excellence, not perfection

62. Stretch your limits

63. Enjoy art

64. Hum a jingle

65. Maintain your weight

66. Plant a tree

67. Feed the birds

68. Practice grace

69. Stretch

70. Have a "plan B"

71. Doodle

72. Learn a joke

73. Know your feelings

74. Meet your needs

75. Know your limits

76. Say "Have a good day," in pig Latin

77. Throw a paper airplane

78. Exercise

79. Learn a new song

80. Get to work earlier

81. Clean a closet

82. Play with a child

83. Go on a picnic

84. Drive a different route to work

85. Leave work early

86. Put air freshener in your car

87. Watch a movie and eat popcorn

88. Write a far-away friend

89. Scream at a ball game

90. Eat a meal by candlelight

91. Recognize the importance of unconditional love

92. Remember stress is an attitude

93. Keep a journal

94. Share a monster smile

95. Remember your options

96. Build a support network

97. Quit trying to fix others

98. Get enough sleep

99. Talk less and listen more

100. Praise others

101. Relax, take each day at a time ... you have the rest of your life to live

Information provided with permission from Kids-in-Touch, a division of West Michigan Addiction Consultants, PC. Phone 616-365-8830 or e-mail www.wemac.com/kit.html.

Section XXVI

SPOUSAL ROLE AND RELATIONSHIP CONFLICT

STATE OF OUR MARRIAGE REPORT

GOALS OF THE EXERCISE

1. Identify areas of spousal harmony and spousal distress.
2. Rate the overall health of the spousal relationship.
3. Agree to improve deficit areas in the marital relationship.
4. Utilize a problem-solving process for resolving marital problems.

ADDITIONAL HOMEWORK THAT MAY BE APPLICABLE
TO SPOUSAL ROLE AND RELATIONSHIP CONFLICT

• Character Development	Sharing the Family Resources	Page 90
• Children with Physical Challenges	Working Together to Create a Plan	Page 102
• Poverty-related Issues	Achieving Family Goals	Page 227
• Prenatal Parenting Preparation	Creating a Family-Friendly Lifestyle	Page 238

ADDITIONAL PROBLEMS THIS EXERCISE MAY BE MOST USEFUL FOR

• Character Development
• Children with Physical Challenges
• Poverty-related Issues
• Prenatal Parenting Preparation

SUGGESTIONS FOR USING THIS EXERCISE WITH PARENTS

The wellness and vitality of a marriage consists of many unique yet interdependent areas of functioning. The couple is directed to rate their marriage in the suggested categories and determine if the overall spousal relationship is good or in need of improvement. The couple then selects one deficit area and uses a problem solving guideline to strengthen the spousal relationship in that area. By working together to improve one aspect of the marriage the couple will find that other areas improve as well. They are cautioned to focus upon one relationship category at a time, to allow the positive momentum of their success to encourage their ongoing efforts to build a happy and enduring marriage.

STATE OF OUR MARRIAGE REPORT

INSTRUCTIONS FOR THE PARENTS

The state of a marriage consists of many separate yet interdependent criteria. Couples usually have an overall view of how their marriage is working, and seldom consider the effectiveness of their marriage in the essential categories that comprise the marriage as a whole. Following is a list of criteria that can be used to evaluate the health of your marriage. Additional categories may be added as needed. Complete the list together or separately and then rate your marriage overall. Discuss each category, and work together to determine which of the weak areas need to be addressed to improve the total marriage.

	Good	Moderate	Needs Work	Comments
Communication				
Conflict resolution				
Discipline				
Emotional support				
Extended family relationships				
Financial goals				
Leisure-time activities				
Parenting effectiveness				
Planning for the future				
Problem-solving				
Respect				
Sexual attraction				
Sexual interaction				
Shared responsibilities				
Social activities				

	Good	Moderate	Needs Work	Comments
Spiritual values				
Spousal relationship				
Tolerance				
Trust				
Our marriage overall				

Agree upon one area that needs work and use the following problem-solving process to create a plan for improvement. By working together to improve the health of your marriage in one category, you will find that other areas show improvement as well. However, you will discover that it is best to keep your focus upon one area at a time to avoid feeling discouraged or overwhelmed. Once your chosen category has improved to a more acceptable level, you can use the positive momentum to deal with another deficit area. Keep working until all categories can be rated in the good to moderate range. Discuss your progress with one another and with your counselor on a weekly basis.

Example:

1. Define the problem or name the category that needs improvement.

    We have very different financial goals. I want to live comfortably now but my spouse wants to save for our future.

2. Brainstorm for solutions.

    * We could keep our separate bank accounts.

    * He can save, I'll spend.

    * We could agree upon a certain amount to save each month and budget for our current expenditures.

    * We could hire a budget consultant.

    * We could read a book about family budgeting and financial fitness (e.g., *The Total Money Makeover* by Dave Ramsey [Thomas Nelson Publishers, 2003]).

3. List the pros and cons of each potential solution.

    * Separate bank accounts will never lead to a consensus about family finances.

    * When he saves and I spend we are always fighting about money.

    * We would both be happier with a designated amount for saving and spending.

    * A budget consultant would help but it would also cost money.

    * Reading about planning a family budget might help us agree upon a financial plan.

4. Choose a potential solution and implement the plan.

    We will buy Dave Ramsey's book and use the guidelines for setting up our family budget. We will designate specific amounts for saving and expenditures.

5. Evaluate the outcome.

    The plan took effort and commitment, but since we reduced our debt we have more money to save and to spend. We are getting along better and the overall state of our marriage seems to have improved. We are ready to tackle another problem area.

STATE OF OUR MARRIAGE PROBLEM-SOLVING WORKSHEET

1. Define the problem or name the category that needs improvement.

    _____

    _____

    _____

    _____

2. Brainstorm for solutions.

    _____

    _____

    _____

    _____

3. List the pros and cons of each potential solution.

    _____

    _____

    _____

    _____

4. Choose a potential solution and implement the plan.

    _____

    _____

    _____

    _____

5. Evaluate the outcome.

    _____

    _____

    _____

    _____

OUR EVOLVING MARRIAGE AND SPOUSAL ROLES

GOALS OF THE EXERCISE

1. Describe current spousal roles and the relationship.
2. Predict how the relationship will evolve over the years.
3. Evaluate how the marriage adjusts to changing circumstances.
4. Prepare for a lifelong spousal relationship.

ADDITIONAL HOMEWORK THAT MAY BE APPLICABLE TO SPOUSAL ROLE AND RELATIONSHIP CONFLICT

- Grandparenting Strategies   Personal Boundaries for Interaction with the Grandchildren   Page 176
- Grief/Loss   Monitoring Our Reactions to Change and Loss   Page 184
- Poverty-related Issues   Achieving Family Goals   Page 227
- Prenatal Parenting Preparation   Creating a Family-Friendly Lifestyle   Page 238

ADDITIONAL PROBLEMS THIS EXERCISE MAY BE MOST USEFUL FOR

- Blended Family
- Grandparenting Strategies
- Grief/Loss
- Poverty-related Issues
- Prenatal Parenting Preparation

SUGGESTIONS FOR USING THIS EXERCISE WITH PARENTS

Marriage is a process that begins with courtship and ends with separation as a result of death or other circumstances that are probably not envisioned or planned for during the early stages of the spousal relationship. This activity directs the parents to view their marriage as a process that will evolve through several stages. By predicting the various joys and challenges they will face, the couple can prepare for their future family and spousal roles and commit to a long-term marriage.

OUR EVOLVING MARRIAGE AND SPOUSAL ROLES

INSTRUCTIONS FOR THE PARENTS

A long-term spousal relationship begins with a friendship or courtship, and ends when the couple is separated due to death or other circumstances. Some marriages won't last that long, but for this activity assume that your marriage is a lifelong commitment. Spousal relationships evolve as the couple matures and circumstances change due to having children, moving, work requirements, social activities, extended family commitments, and physical changes. Envisioning and planning for the current and future needs of your marriage and family will help you prepare for the changing roles and requirements you will face as partners in a lifelong spousal relationship.

Begin when you first met and describe the various aspects of your relationship, using the following list. Continue through the stages of marriage, and either describe or predict how your marriage evolves due to the circumstances and demands of each stage. By envisioning your marriage in the long term you will prepare yourselves for the joys and challenges of a lifelong spousal relationship.

Stages of a Spousal Relationship

Courtship:

Relationship: _____

_____

Roles: _____

_____

Responsibilities: _____

_____

_____

Problems: _____

_____

_____

_____

Social activities and hobbies: _____

_____

_____

Problem-solving strategies: _____

_____

_____

Rewards and joys of the relationship: _____

_____

_____

_____

Financial status, obligations, problems: _____

_____

_____

Additional comments: _____

_____

_____

_____

First Seven Years of Marriage:

Relationship: _____

_____

Roles: _____

_____

Responsibilities: _____

_____

_____

Children's ages and stages: _____

_____

_____

_____

Problems: _____

_____

_____

_____

Social activities and hobbies: _____

_____

_____

_____

Problem-solving strategies: _____

_____

_____

_____

Rewards and joys of the relationship: _____

_____

_____

_____

Financial status, obligations, problems: _____

_____

_____

_____

Additional comments: _____

_____

_____

_____

Second Seven Years of Marriage:

Relationship: _____

_____

Roles: _____

_____

Responsibilities: _____

_____

_____

Children's ages and stages: _____

_____

_____

_____

Problems: _____

_____

_____

_____

Social activities and hobbies: _____

_____

_____

_____

Problem-solving strategies: _____

_____

_____

_____

Rewards and joys of the relationship: _____

_____

_____

_____

Financial status, obligations, problems: _____

_____

_____

_____

Additional comments: _____

_____

_____

_____

Third Seven Years of Marriage:

Relationship: _____

_____

Roles: _____

_____

Responsibilities: _____

_____

Children's ages and stages: _____

_____

Problems: _____

_____

Social activities and hobbies: _____

_____

Problem-solving strategies: _____

_____

_____

_____

Rewards and joys of the relationship: _____

_____

_____

_____

Financial status, obligations, problems: _____

_____

_____

_____

Additional comments: _____

_____

_____

_____

The Empty Nest Years:

Relationship: _____

_____

Roles: _____

_____

Responsibilities: _____

_____

_____

Children's ages and stages: _____

_____

_____

_____

Problems: _____

_____

_____

_____

Social activities and hobbies: _____

_____

_____

Problem-solving strategies: _____

_____

_____

_____

Rewards and joys of the relationship: _____

_____

_____

_____

Financial status, obligations, problems: _____

_____

_____

_____

Additional comments: _____

_____

_____

_____

Grandparenting and Beyond:

Relationship: _____

_____

Roles: _____

_____

Responsibilities: _____

_____

_____

Grandchildren's ages and stages: _____

_____

_____

_____

Problems: _____

_____

_____

Social activities and hobbies: _____

_____

_____

_____

Problem-solving strategies: _____

_____

_____

Rewards and joys of the relationship: _____

_____

_____

Financial status, obligations, problems: _____

_____

_____

_____

Additional comments: _____

_____

_____

STRATEGIES FOR PRESCHOOLERS (AGES BIRTH TO 6)

CHARTING OUR CHILD'S DEVELOPMENTAL STAGES

GOALS OF THE EXERCISE

1. Assess the child's developmental milestones.
2. Chart the child's developmental levels during the preschool years.
3. Determine which factors contribute to the child's developmental status.
4. Identify interventions to enhance and encourage the child's normal developmental growth in all areas.

ADDITIONAL HOMEWORK THAT MAY BE APPLICABLE
FOR ENCOURAGING DEVELOPMENTAL GROWTH

• Bonding/Attachment Issues	The Behavior Progress Chart	Page 64
• Children with Physical Challenges	Strategies for Supporting Our Child with Physical Challenges	Page 100
• Strategies for Children (Ages 7 to 12)	Record of Reinforced Behavior	Page 319
• Poverty-related Issues	Achieving Family Goals	Page 227

ADDITIONAL PROBLEMS THIS EXERCISE MAY BE MOST USEFUL FOR

• Bonding/Attachment Issues
• Attention-seeking Behavior
• Children with Physical Challenges
• Strategies for Children
• Poverty-related Issues

SUGGESTIONS FOR USING THIS EXERCISE WITH FAMILIES

Parents frequently worry about their child's developmental milestones and wonder if they are normal or delayed. This activity directs the parents to record developmental levels of growth, beginning with the child's birth, throughout the preschool years, and beyond. This information is extremely useful during medical and educational assessments and helps the parents to identify the child's overall pattern of maturation. The parents are guided to evaluate various developmental levels every six months and to determine the contributing factors influencing the child's behavior. Interventions to address delayed development and to support average and advanced milestones can be determined by the parents alone or with the assistance of the child's doctor, counselor, or teacher.

CHARTING OUR CHILD'S DEVELOPMENTAL STAGES

INSTRUCTIONS FOR THE PARENTS

Children go through developmental stages from the time of conception through early adulthood. The developmental process is faster and more apparent during the early childhood stages and slows down as the child reaches the late teens. With each stage come new physical, mental, emotional, and social accomplishments and challenges. Children develop according to their own schedules; however, generic milestones have been established by physicians, psychologists, and educators to help parents track their child's maturation and determine if it is within the normal range, advanced, or behind schedule.

Charting your child's progress from the earliest stages through young adulthood will help you recognize the current level of development and determine if there are any problematic delays that need to be addressed. Children often develop unevenly, and are precocious in some areas while average or delayed in others. Record your child's current levels of functioning in the following areas and indicate if the child's milestones are advanced, average, or delayed, compared to other children of the same age. If you're not sure how to rate specific developmental levels, check with the child's pediatrician, teacher, or counselor. Next, consider the factors that contribute to the child's developmental status (e.g., premature birth, physical problems, and overparenting can contribute to developmental delays; preschool, a nutritious diet, an emotionally stable environment, and caring parental interaction can contribute to average or advanced behavior and learning). Then determine what, if any, interventions should be taken to address the child's developmental delays or to support and encourage normal development.

Continue to chart your child's developmental progress about every six months—throughout the preschool years and beyond—to establish a record of important developmental milestones. This record will be a useful guide as your child progresses through preschool and prepares for the many challenges and opportunities experienced by school-aged children.

Example:

Child's name: Charlie   Child's age: 18 months

Developmental Behavior	Status (Advanced, Average, Delayed)	Contributing Factors	Action To Be Taken
Bonding/attachment	Advanced	Frequent loving parent/child interaction	Continue to encourage
Gross motor skills	Average	Good natural ability	Continue to encourage
Fine motor skills	Average	Parents encourage fine motor tasks	Continue to encourage
Emotional expression	Advanced	Parents model appropriate emotional expression	Continue to teach and model
Social interaction	Delayed	Little interaction with other children	Set up regular interaction with other children
Cognitive ability	Advanced	Good natural ability	Encourage innate desire to learn
Character development	Average	Parents encourage appropriate behavior	Continue to encourage
Communication skills	Advanced	Frequent parent/child communication	Continue frequent loving parent interaction
Physical health	Average	Regular health checkups	Continue checkups

Child's name: _____   Child's age: _____

Developmental Behavior	Status (Advanced, Average, Delayed)	Contributing Factors	Action To Be Taken
Bonding/attachment			
Gross motor skills			
Fine motor skills			
Emotional expression			
Social interaction			
Cognitive ability			
Character development			
Communication skills			
Physical health			

Child's name: _____ Child's age: _____

Developmental Behavior	Status (Advanced, Average, Delayed)	Contributing Factors	Action To Be Taken
Bonding/attachment			
Gross motor skills			
Fine motor skills			
Emotional expression			
Social interaction			
Cognitive ability			
Character development			
Communication skills			
Physical health			

Child's name: _____ Child's age: _____

Developmental Behavior	Status (Advanced, Average, Delayed)	Contributing Factors	Action To Be Taken
Bonding/attachment			
Gross motor skills			
Fine motor skills			
Emotional expression			
Social interaction			
Cognitive ability			
Character development			
Communication skills			
Physical health			

Child's name: _____ Child's age: _____

Developmental Behavior	Status (Advanced, Average, Delayed)	Contributing Factors	Action To Be Taken
Bonding/attachment			
Gross motor skills			
Fine motor skills			
Emotional expression			
Social interaction			
Cognitive ability			
Character development			
Communication skills			
Physical health			

HELPING MY CHILD DEVELOP
RESPONSIBLE BEHAVIOR

GOALS OF THE EXERCISE

1. Teach new skills to the child.
2. Encourage cooperation and independent behavior.
3. Affirm the child's attempts to learn new skills.
4. Encourage the child to develop responsible behavior.

ADDITIONAL HOMEWORK THAT MAY BE APPLICABLE
FOR ENCOURAGING DEVELOPMENTAL GROWTH

• Attention-Deficit/Hyperactivity Disorder (ADHD)	Family Problem Resolution Worksheet	Page 29
• Bonding/Attachment Issues	Steps to Responsible Behavior	Page 60
• Gifted/Talented	Teaching Responsibility	Page 162
• Poverty-related Issues	Achieving Family Goals	Page 227

ADDITIONAL PROBLEMS THIS EXERCISE MAY BE MOST USEFUL FOR

- Bonding/Attachment Issues
- Attention-Deficit/Hyperactivity Disorder (ADHD)
- Children with Physical Challenges
- Strategies for Children
- Poverty-related Issues

SUGGESTIONS FOR USING THIS EXERCISE WITH FAMILIES

This activity guides the parents to help their preschooler develop more responsible and age-appropriate behavior, by determining several skills to teach their child and then focusing on one new task or responsibility each week. The parents select one task to teach the child and determine the strategies they will use to encourage and affirm the child's positive attempts to learn the skill and the can-do messages and consequences with empathy that can be used to redirect the child's efforts toward the goal. The child's responsibility chart can be kept as an ongoing record of the preschooler's progress toward growth, maturity, and independent behavior.

HELPING MY CHILD DEVELOP RESPONSIBLE BEHAVIOR

INSTRUCTIONS FOR THE PARENTS

Encourage your preschooler to develop responsible behavior by assigning one new responsibility or challenge each month that is age appropriate and well within the child's ability level. Create a responsibility chart that will track the preschooler's accomplishments and will become an ongoing record of the child's progress toward growth, maturity, and responsibility. Celebrate the child's mastery of each new task by reviewing the chart together and affirming the positive growth.

Begin by brainstorming the tasks, chores, and responsibilities you hope your preschooler will accomplish during the next month. Then, choose one task to focus on and record it on the following chart. Teach the child how to complete one selected task each week by modeling and demonstrating the steps involved and by offering assistance while the child learns the new skill. Use encouragement when the child is making a positive effort to learn the new task and affirm each step toward mastery. Use logical consequences, with empathy, and use can-do messages when the preschooler becomes uncooperative or oppositional and tries to avoid the task or responsibility being taught.

Example:

Child's name: Jerome   Age or ability level: 3 years

Tasks or responsibilities we will assign our child during the next month:

1. To put on his coat by himself.

2. To brush his teeth by himself.

3. To pick up his toys before dinner.

4. To say his prayers at night before bedtime.

Assigned weekly task:

To put on his coat by himself.

Methods we will use to teach the task:

Demonstrate putting coat on one arm at a time.

Demonstrate how to button or zip up the coat.

Demonstrate how to lay the coat on the floor and flip it on over his head.

Help him while he learns how to put on his coat and zip or button it up.

Consequences and strategies we will use if the task is not completed satisfactorily:

Give him a choice of which coat to wear.

Ask him if he wants to put it on alone or with help.

Tell him we can't leave until his coat is on.

Have him start in plenty of time to complete the job.

Say he needs to stay in his room until his coat is on.

Tell him no toys or TV until his coat is on.

Tell him he can't play outside until his coat is on.

Say, "Jerome, I know you can put your coat on all by yourself or with just a little help."

Encouragement and affirmations we will use to reinforce task completion:

"You're learning to zip or button all by yourself!"

"Jerome, you put that coat on so fast!"

"You must feel really proud when you put your coat on all by yourself!"

"We'll have extra time to play now since you put your coat on right away."

"I'm going to call Grandma and tell her that you can put your coat on all by yourself."

MY PRESCHOOLER'S RESPONSIBILITY CHART

Child's name: _____   Age or ability level: _____

Tasks or responsibilities we will assign our child during the next month:

1. _____

2. _____

3. _____

4. _____

Assigned weekly task:

_____

Methods we will use to teach the task:

_____

_____

_____

Consequences and strategies we will use if the task is not completed satisfactorily:

_____

_____

_____

Encouragement and affirmations we will use to reinforce task completion:

_____

_____

_____

Assigned weekly task:

_____

Methods we will use to teach the task:

_____

_____

_____

Consequences and strategies we will use if the task is not completed satisfactorily:

_____

_____

_____

Encouragement and affirmations we will use to reinforce task completion:

_____

_____

_____

Assigned weekly task:

_____

Methods we will use to teach the task:

_____

_____

_____

Consequences and strategies we will use if the task is not completed satisfactorily:

_____

_____

_____

Encouragement and affirmations we will use to reinforce task completion:

_____

_____

_____

Assigned weekly task:

_____

Methods we will use to teach the task:

_____

_____

_____

Consequences and strategies we will use if the task is not completed satisfactorily:

_____

_____

_____

Encouragement and affirmations we will use to reinforce task completion:

_____

_____

_____

Assigned weekly task:

_____

Methods we will use to teach the task:

_____

_____

_____

Consequences and strategies we will use if the task is not completed satisfactorily:

_____

_____

_____

Encouragement and affirmations we will use to reinforce task completion:

_____

_____

_____

STRATEGIES FOR CHILDREN
(AGES 7 TO 12)

THE REWIND GAME

GOALS OF THE EXERCISE

1. Identify inappropriate personal behavior and responses that upset and frustrate others.
2. Rewrite inappropriate responses in positive terms.
3. Practice using appropriate behavior and responses with others.
4. Control impulsive, negative responses, and replace them with positive actions.

ADDITIONAL HOMEWORK THAT MAY BE APPLICABLE TO DEVELOPING APPROPRIATE BEHAVIOR

• Attention-Deficit/ Hyperactivity Disorder (ADHD)	Family Problem Resolution Worksheet	Page 29
• Posttraumatic Stress Disorder (PTSD)	Reframing Our Worries	Page 216
• Single Parenting	Stress Reduction Strategies	Page 276
• Spousal Role and Relationship Conflict	State of Our Marriage Report	Page 282

ADDITIONAL PROBLEMS THIS EXERCISE MAY BE MOST USEFUL FOR

• Attention-Deficit/Hyperactivity Disorder (ADHD)
• Blended Family
• Posttraumatic Stress Disorder (PTSD)
• Single Parenting
• Spousal Role and Relationship Conflict

SUGGESTIONS FOR USING THIS EXERCISE WITH FAMILIES

Parents and children who react or behave impulsively can benefit from looking at their actions and considering how they would behave if given another opportunity. "The Rewind Game" instructs the family members to describe a scenario from personal experience, identify an action that created a problem either for oneself or for another person, and then to rewrite the inappropriate response in more positive terms. This process will help the child understand that there are both appropriate and inappropriate methods of responding to any situation; positive responses contribute to positive relationships and results, whereas negative responses create undesirable consequences. It also provides an opportunity for the parents to model problem-solving and remorseful responses when a thoughtless or inappropriate gesture has created distress for a valued family member, friend, or colleague.

THE REWIND GAME

INSTRUCTIONS FOR THE PARENT AND THE CHILD

Family members often say or do things that they regret, and wish that they had the opportunity to rewind and try again. "The Rewind Game" allows both parents and children to restate or redo an inappropriate comment or behavior and resolve a problem or issue with someone who was hurt or upset by their initial words or actions. In the following space describe several situations that created problems or hurt feelings, describe what was actually said or done, and suggest a more appropriate rewind version. Finally, show this activity sheet to the other involved person and ask permission to respond more appropriately.

Play the rewind game as a family. Each player receives 5 points for describing a situation and creating a rewind version on the activity sheet. Score 10 points for each situation that a player is able to rewind with the other affected person. 0 to 10 points indicates that the player is a rewind beginner, 10 to 30 points indicates an intermediate level rewind player, 30 or more points indicates that the player is developing expert rewind skills.

Examples:

Situation	What I Said or Did	My Rewind Version
I wanted my mom to drive me home from school and she said she would be a few minutes late.	I blew up when she picked me up and called her selfish. I told her she didn't care about me and didn't love me. She said my words made her not want to pick me up at all.	I will tell my mom that I get frustrated when she doesn't pick me up on time and that I am sorry for my hurtful words. I will thank her for taking the time to pick me up when I ask.
I told my dad I would be home on time for dinner.	I watched a video with a friend and completely lost track of the time. I was an hour late for dinner. My dad said I couldn't go out for the rest of the week.	Next time, I will be sure to wear a watch or check a clock so I make it home on time for dinner.
I promised Tobias that I would come to his football game Friday night and take his friends out for a treat afterwards.	I got involved in an emergency work project and totally forgot to attend the game. Tobias was angry and disappointed that I had let him and his friends down.	I will explain the situation to Tobias and apologize for not contacting him about my change in plans. I will try to make it up to him by rescheduling with him and his friends for the next two home games.

The Rewind Game

Situation	What I Said or Did	My Rewind Version

RECORD OF REINFORCED BEHAVIOR

GOALS OF THE EXERCISE

1. Identify the child's inappropriate behavior.
2. Determine the factors that are reinforcing the child's negative behavior.
3. Identify the mistaken goals of the child's misbehavior.
4. Plan interventions that will encourage and reinforce the child's appropriate behavior.

ADDITIONAL HOMEWORK THAT MAY BE APPLICABLE TO ADDRESSING INAPPROPRIATE BEHAVIOR

• Attention-seeking Behavior	Family Problem Resolution Worksheet	Page 29
• Bonding/Attachment Issues	The Behavior Progress Chart	Page 64
• Children with Physical Challenges	Working Together to Create a Plan	Page 102
• Conduct Disorder/ Delinquent Behavior	Replacing Noncompliance with Compliance and Cooperation	Page 109

ADDITIONAL PROBLEMS THIS EXERCISE MAY BE MOST USEFUL FOR

*   Attention-seeking Behavior
*   Bonding/Attachment Issues
*   Career Preparation
*   Children with Physical Challenges

SUGGESTIONS FOR USING THIS EXERCISE WITH FAMILIES

The "Record of Reinforced Behavior" is to be used by the parents, with the help of a counselor, to evaluate the child's inappropriate or dysfunctional behavior and plan for specific intervention strategies that will encourage positive alternative behaviors. Parents often reinforce their child's negative behavior with reactions that actually feed into the child's subconscious motivations for misbehavior. By identifying the underlying goals the parents can begin to meet the child's needs, by reinforcing positive behavior and by using strategies of positive discipline to extinguish negative behavior.

RECORD OF REINFORCED BEHAVIOR

INSTRUCTIONS FOR THE PARENTS

Children misbehave for four reasons: attention, power, revenge, and fear of failure (see *Children: The Challenge,* by Dreikurs and Stolz [Plume, 1990]); parents often reinforce negative behavior by unconsciously or inadvertently reacting in ways that feed into the child's mistaken motivations. Parents can begin to eliminate this unhelpful cycle by defining their current reactions to the child's inappropriate behavior and by substituting a more effective response that encourages the child to attain his or her goals through positive rather than negative actions.

Use the Record of Reinforced Behavior chart to create a plan for addressing the child's misbehavior. Begin by listing the behaviors of concern in the first column. Use specific descriptors (e.g., arguing, interrupting, whining, hitting, refusal to do chores) rather than generalizations (e.g., inattention, rudeness, lack of follow through). Complete the second column by listing all the possible factors that may be encouraging the inappropriate behavior. These will be reactions from you as parents, other family members, teachers, and significant others. Then use the third column to identify the child's mistaken goals of misbehavior or the reward being sought from engaging in the negative behavior (e.g., attention, power, revenge, or fear of failure).

Plan for intervention strategies by considering the goals of the misbehavior and by determining how to help the child meet these goals, using positive rather than negative behavior. If the child is seeking attention, how can this goal be met through cooperative, socially appropriate, and productive behavior? List some techniques of positive discipline (e.g., consequences, encouragement, choices, enforceable limits, "I"-statements) in the fourth column that will encourage the child's positive behavior and will eliminate the reinforcement of the existing negative behavior. Describe the outcome of the interventions in the fifth column. Keep an ongoing record of the strategies that do and do not work and revise the planned interventions as needed.

Example:

Date: January 15 to January 31   Child's name: Tanecia   Parents: Jarrod and Lillian

Negative Behaviors	Reinforcing Factors	Child's Goals	Planned Interventions	Outcome
Interrupting when I'm on the phone.	I nag her to stop. I give her the evil eye. I put the phone down and lecture her. I give her something to eat. I tell her I'll help her in a minute. I get her what she wants.	Attention Power	Ask Tanecia not to interrupt. Give her a choice of playing quietly or going to her room. Hang up and send her to her room when she interrupts. Put her in her room before making the next phone call. Give her a chance to not interrupt the next day. Limit time on the phone and give Tanecia more positive attention when she is behaving appropriately.	Tanecia is much more respectful since I follow through with choices and consequences and give her more attention for positive behavior.

Record of Reinforced Behavior

Date: _____ Child's name: _____ Age: _____

Parents: _____ _____

Negative Behaviors	Reinforcing Factors	Child's Goals	Planned Interventions	Outcome

PROBLEM-SOLVING WORKSHEET

GOALS OF THE EXERCISE

1. The child identifies inappropriate personal behavior.
2. Increase the child's awareness of the effects of misbehavior on self and others.
3. The child develops cause-and-effect thinking.
4. The child recognizes appropriate solutions to behavioral problems.

ADDITIONAL HOMEWORK THAT MAY BE APPLICABLE TO HELPING CHILDREN RESOLVE PROBLEMS

• Attention-seeking Behavior	Family Job Support Checklist	Page 37
• Conduct Disorder/ Delinquent Behavior	Using Privileges as Contingencies and Consequences	Page 114
• Dependent Children/ Overprotective Parent	Overprotective Parent versus Positive Parent	Page 120
• Oppositional Defiant Disorder (ODD)	Planning for Disruptive Behavior	Page 194

ADDITIONAL PROBLEMS THIS EXERCISE MAY BE MOST USEFUL FOR

- Attention-Deficit/Hyperactivity Disorder (ADHD)
- Conduct Disorder/Delinquent Behavior
- Dependent Children/Overprotective Parent
- Oppositional Defiant Disorder (ODD)

SUGGESTIONS FOR USING THIS EXERCISE WITH FAMILIES

It is useful to involve the child in designing a consequence or remedy whenever his or her inappropriate behavior creates a problem. This process allows the child to recognize that violating the personal guidelines of *regard, respect,* and *responsibility* has a negative impact on both self and others. The problem-solving worksheet guides the child to resolve the problem by identifying the inappropriate behavior and then relating it to a guideline for positive character development. The child then creates a plan for a consequence or remedy that will provide a meaningful learning opportunity, and develops a list of appropriate behaviors to use the next time a similar situation occurs. The problem-solving worksheet should be completed before the child is allowed to engage in any activities where a similar problem might occur.

PROBLEM-SOLVING WORKSHEET

INSTRUCTIONS FOR THE PARENTS

Developing a plan to solve a problem that the child has created can encourage the child to learn from a mistake and to figure out a better way to deal with a similar situation next time. When the children help to determine appropriate consequences or remedies for a problem that they have created, the result is much more positive than when a parent or teacher tries to figure out a solution without input from the child.

Address the problem by finding a quiet place where the child can think about the problem without too many distractions. Then, assign the child to complete the worksheet by writing down as much information as possible about the situation that needs to be resolved.

Children can be quite fair and appropriate when asked to examine their own behavior, and the consequence or remedy they suggest is often very effective, because:

- They become invested in the plan.

- They know what works best with them.

- They would rather design a consequence than have an adult do it for them.

If the child's plan is incomplete, inadequate, or inappropriate, the parent or counselor always reserves the right to substitute a different consequence or remedy.

INSTRUCTIONS FOR THE CHILD

Complete the problem-solving worksheet by answering each question fully, using the back of the paper and/or additional paper if necessary.

What Happened?

First, it is important to determine what happened. This means what was going on right before the problem occurred, which may have contributed to the problem. What were you doing or saying, or what were you thinking? What were others that were involved doing or saying? Write down anything that occurred which you think should be part of explaining what happened.

Which Guideline Did I Ignore?

The guidelines for appropriate behavior and social success include regard, respect, and responsibility for self and others. All behaviors that cause problems are related to one of these guidelines.

Examples:

- Jim hits his sister on the way to school *(regard)*.

- Jerry will not participate in cleaning up the family room *(responsibility)*.

- Susie calls her brother names *(respect)*.

- Jenny draws pictures on the bathroom wall *(respect, responsibility)*.

- Josh calls his father, "Mr. Turkey" *(respect)*.

- Danell throws food on the floor *(responsibility)*.

- Ellen talks back to her mother *(respect)*.

Determine which guideline you ignored when the problem occurred. Write it down in the space provided.

How Did My Behavior Cause a Problem for Someone Else?

Inappropriate behavior usually causes a problem for others, such as your parents, teachers, siblings, or classmates. Who was directly affected in a negative way by your problem behavior? Write down the names of the affected people and how the behavior caused them difficulty.

How Did My Behavior Cause A Problem For Me?

All problem behavior eventually causes a problem for you. What kinds of consequences, hassles, struggles, or frustrations are you now dealing with as a result of your behavior or mistake? Write your ideas down in this section of the worksheet.

My Plan for a Consequence or Remedy

The best way to handle a mistake or problem is to think of a consequence that will make sure that the same behavior will not happen again and to fix any damage or hurt done to another person. Look at what you have written in the "How Did My Behavior Cause a Problem for Someone Else" section. Decide how you can make things right with the person or people who were affected. Then decide what will teach you a different and more appropriate way of behaving. Think of a consequence that will help you remember not to behave in ways that hurt you or someone else. The consequence should be powerful enough to help you change your behavior. Try to make the consequence fit the problem (e.g., if the problem occurred at bedtime, then the consequence could be to go to bed earlier the next evening and think about what happened; or, if the problem involved hurting or disrespecting a sibling, the consequence or remedy could be to help that sibling in a way that builds a more positive relationship). You are the most important part of the consequence or remedy. Make sure to think of something that will make a real difference for you.

Next Time

It's impossible to get rid of a negative behavior unless you have a positive behavior to replace it with. Possibly you already know what you wish you would have done instead of using an inappropriate behavior. Now is your chance to plan for what you want to do next time. Possibly you will use words instead of hitting, or use respectful language to ask a question or make a comment. Think of as many positive ways as possible to deal with a similar situation. Write all of your ideas down and pick one or two to use next time. If you need help with this part be sure to ask your parents, counselor, or another family member for input.

When you have completed this worksheet share it with your parents or counselor. They will want to discuss it with you to make sure it is complete and has a good chance for success. It may take one or two attempts to come up with a plan that will work, but the positive results in developing regard, respect, and responsibility for self and others is well worth your time and effort. Good luck!

PROBLEM-SOLVING WORKSHEET

Personal Guidelines:

- Regard for self and others
- Respect for self and others
- Responsibility to self and others

What happened?

_____

_____

_____

Which guideline did I ignore?

_____

How did my behavior cause a problem for someone else?

_____

_____

_____

How did my behavior cause a problem for me?

_____

_____

My plan for a consequence or remedy is:

_____

_____

Next time I plan to:

_____

_____

_____

Name: _____ Date: _____

Parent's or counselor's name: _____

Section XXIX

STRATEGIES FOR TEENAGERS
(AGES 13 TO 18)

LISTENING WITH EMPATHY

GOALS OF THE EXERCISE

1. Verbalize a definition of effective listening.
2. Identify the feelings expressed during a conversation.
3. Acquire techniques necessary for becoming an active listener.
4. Acknowledge the credibility of the teenager's feelings.

ADDITIONAL HOMEWORK THAT MAY BE APPLICABLE TO EMPATHETIC LISTENING

ADDITIONAL PROBLEMS THIS EXERCISE MAY BE MOST USEFUL FOR

- Attention-seeking Behavior
- Grief/Loss
- Sibling Rivalry
- Substance Abuse
- Suicide Prevention

SUGGESTIONS FOR USING THIS EXERCISE WITH FAMILIES

Parents often view communication with their children as self-expression or "talking" and giving advice. This activity is designed to teach the sometimes forgotten aspect of communication: *listening*. The parents are introduced to the five components of active listening: eye contact, paraphrasing, reflecting the feeling being expressed, remaining nonjudgmental, and waiting until asked to give advice. An inventory of "feeling" words is provided and can be used to identify the feelings expressed in the examples listed. The parents are then directed to select a feeling that would appropriately reflect the child's emotions based on the information given in each example. This activity helps parents focus on their child's feelings and open the lines of communication, using empathy and interest in the teen's point of view.

LISTENING WITH EMPATHY

INSTRUCTIONS FOR THE PARENTS

Learning to listen to your children and other members of your family actively and with empathy is a skill that is developed through a lot of practice. This skill is particularly effective for communicating with teens and helping them sort through the variety of situations and emotions that are experienced during this volatile stage of life.

This activity defines the five essential strategies of effective listening, and directs the parents to respond to several situations where active listening would be an appropriate and effective response. Perhaps your teenager tells you about something that has made him or her feel sad or unhappy. You would respond with the word that describes the feeling you imagine is being experienced at that moment. Or, your teenager is letting you know about something wonderful that is about to happen. You could recognize the feelings of excitement by responding with a feeling word that reflects the joy they are expressing.

Discuss and role-play five components of being a good listener with your family counselor. Review the feeling words listed and add any additional words that describe feelings commonly experienced by you, your teen, and other members of your family. Then complete the responses to the following statements by choosing a feeling word that reflects the feeling being expressed about an event that is affecting the teen's attitude or emotions. Continue to practice using feeling words to respond to conversations with your teen and other family members; you will find that they recognize your listening talents, and seek you out often to share their feelings and experiences and welcome your input.

A Good Listener Tries To:

1. Look at the person who is speaking.

2. Remember and be able to repeat back important details.

3. Identify how the person is feeling.

4. Remain nonjudgmental throughout the conversation.

5. Give advice only when requested.

Read the list of feeling words and add several of your own.

angry	embarrassed	jealous	surprised
anxious	enraged	lonely	suspicious
ashamed	excited	lovestruck	_____
bored	exhausted	mischievous	_____
cautious	frightened	overwhelmed	_____
confident	frustrated	sad	_____
confused	guilty	serious	_____
depressed	happy	shocked	_____
disgusted	hopeful	shy	_____
ecstatic	hysterical	smug	_____

Choose a word from the list above that reflects the feeling being communicated in each of the following situations.

Your teen tells you a friend is seriously ill and in the hospital.

Response: *You're feeling very* _____.

Your teen has just told a joke that made you laugh.

Response: *That is really* _____.

Your teen is complaining that he lost his homework.

Response: *You sound like you're* _____.

The teacher is explaining important instructions for the test.

Response: *Remain quiet and look* _____.

Your teen says he's won a poster contest at school.

Response: *You must be very* _____.

Record several emotional comments your teen has made and create a response that uses active and empathetic listening. Continue to use the rules of effective communication with your teenager and other family members; note their increased willingness to continue the conversation and explore a range of feelings when you remain nonjudgmental and compassionate.

Comment: _____

_____

Response: *You sound very* _____.

Comment: _____

_____

Response: *You sound very* _____.

Comment: _____

_____

Response: *You sound very* _____.

Comment: _____

_____

Response: *You sound very* _____.

Comment: _____

_____

Response: *You sound very* _____.

Comment: _____

_____

Response: *You sound very* _____.

Comment: _____

_____

Response: *You sound very* _____.

Comment: _____

_____

Response: *You sound very* _____.

Comment: _____

_____

Response: *You sound very* _____.

EARNING PRIVILEGES AND FREEDOMS

GOALS OF THE EXERCISE

1. Identify areas where the teen is demonstrating responsibility.
2. Designate behavioral areas where parental monitoring is necessary.
3. List privileges and freedoms that are contingent upon the teen's responsible behavior.
4. Determine the steps necessary to reduce parental monitoring.

ADDITIONAL HOMEWORK THAT MAY BE APPLICABLE TO FAMILIES WITH TEENAGERS

• Bonding/Attachment Issues	Steps to Responsible Behavior	Page 60
• Conduct Disorder/ Delinquent Behavior	Using Privileges as Contingencies and Consequences	Page 114
• Sexual Responsibility	My Personal Sexual Responsibility Code	Page 262
• Suicide Prevention	Heart-to-Heart Smart Talks	Page 354

ADDITIONAL PROBLEMS THIS EXERCISE MAY BE MOST USEFUL FOR

- Bonding/Attachment Issues
- Children with Physical Challenges
- Conduct Disorder/Delinquent Behavior
- Eating Disorder
- Sexual Responsibility

SUGGESTIONS FOR USING THIS EXERCISE WITH FAMILIES

Teens are often anxious to manage their own schoolwork, grades, dating, curfew, driving, health-related issues, and other areas of responsibility without their parents' interference. However, parents feel an obligation to monitor performance in critical areas of functioning until the teen has demonstrated a record of maturity and reliability. This activity suggests that many of the privileges and freedoms desired by teens should be earned by establishing an acceptable level of performance, and that parental monitoring should be reduced only after the teen demonstrates the ability to function independently. The parents and the teen are directed to complete a chart that lists several areas where parental monitoring is still required. Then, the privileges and freedoms associated with the teen's positive performance are established along with the conditions under which parental monitoring can be reduced. The chart should be maintained until parental monitoring in most areas is no longer necessary.

EARNING PRIVILEGES AND FREEDOMS

INSTRUCTIONS FOR THE PARENTS AND THE TEENAGER

The teen years are ideal for learning about consequences and the laws of cause and effect. In just a few short years the teen will leave home and enter a world in which positive personal efforts and actions result in positive outcomes, and negative personal behavior and lack of effort create very disappointing results. If the child can learn this important lesson as a teenager or even younger, the transition to the consequential world of adulthood will be much smoother and less painful.

The parent's role is to extend privileges and freedoms to the child when responsibility and independence have been demonstrated, and to withhold them when the teen's behavior is immature and inappropriate. Parental monitoring of chores, homework, curfew, dating, abstinence from harmful substances, and other responsibilities is necessary until the teen is able to handle each life skill fully—without being reminded. Once appropriate independent functioning has been demonstrated, the level of parental supervision can be reduced. Teens often resent being monitored too closely. However, being able to handle a responsibility independently is a privilege and a freedom that should be earned by demonstrating an appropriate level of independent functioning.

Work together to create a list of teen behaviors and expectations that currently receive your parental monitoring. Indicate the privileges and freedoms that are contingent upon the teen's responsible actions in each area. Then, indicate what the teen will need to do to earn each privilege and freedom and reduce or eliminate the need for parental monitoring in that area.

Continue to use the chart to record areas of the teen's responsibilities that require parental supervision until the need for parental responsibility has been eliminated in all areas.

Example:

Area of Responsibility	Associated Privileges and Freedoms	Steps Necessary to Reduce Parental Monitoring
Driving an automobile	Driving the family car with supervision	Take driver's education
	Driving alone	Drive 500 supervised miles
	Driving with friends in the car	Acquire a driver's license
	Driving to school	Pay half of the additional insurance
	Driving at night	Drive accident free
	Driving out of town	Drive alcohol and drug free
		Pay for the gasoline used

RESPONSIBILITY, PRIVILEGES, FREEDOMS, AND PARENTAL MONITORING CHART

Area of Responsibility	Associated Privileges and Freedoms	Steps Necessary to Reduce Parental Monitoring

Section XXX

SUBSTANCE ABUSE

HEALTHY HABITS TO SUPPORT RECOVERY

GOALS OF THE EXERCISE

1. Define threats to recovery.
2. Identify antidotes to prevent a relapse of substance abuse.
3. Define a plan for recovery
4. Abstain from substance abuse.

ADDITIONAL HOMEWORK THAT MAY BE APPLICABLE TO SUBSTANCE ABUSE

• Abusive Parenting	Our Family's Secret Story	Page 5
• Prenatal Parenting Preparation	Creating a Family-Friendly Lifestyle	Page 238
• Sexual Responsibility	Sexual Responsibility and Healthy Self-esteem	Page 258
• Suicide Prevention	Heart-to-Heart Smart Talks	Page 354

ADDITIONAL PROBLEMS THIS EXERCISE MAY BE MOST USEFUL FOR

- Abusive Parenting
- Prenatal Parenting Preparation
- Sexual Responsibility
- Strategies for Teenagers
- Suicide Prevention

SUGGESTIONS FOR USING THIS EXERCISE WITH FAMILIES

The road to recovery is long and hard for children who have become addicted to harmful substances. This activity is designed to help the parents and the chemical-dependent child to recognize the healthy habits that can avert temptations and promote a substance-free lifestyle. Numerous healthy habits and behaviors that can support the child's commitment to remain substance-free are listed. The parents and the child are asked to add some additional strategies that can defend against the powerful pull of addiction and related behaviors. The family members are reminded that it is nearly impossible to give up an unhealthy habit unless a healthy habit is substituted.

After reviewing the antidotes to relapse, parents and the child are instructed to define some actual temptations or danger zones for the child and to choose a healthy habit to combat a relapse to addictive behavior. The child is directed to identify the most helpful strategy, a primary empathetic personal resource, and a major motivating factor for committing to a substance-free lifestyle.

HEALTHY HABITS TO SUPPORT RECOVERY

INSTRUCTIONS FOR THE PARENTS AND THE CHILD

There are many antidotes to help parents and their substance-using child prevent a relapse to chemical dependence. Experienced support systems exist to guide families in their journey toward recovery. These include private therapists, school programs, religious groups, and community agencies, which are willing and able to offer the empathy, encouragement, and guidance necessary to overcome chemical dependence. The most important resource is the commitment of the chemical-dependent child and the support of loving parents and other family members. Once a determination is made to live substance-free the child will discover that others are anxious to offer real assistance.

Following is a list of positive habits and behaviors that will greatly assist families in their efforts to support the child's substance-free lifestyle. Addiction is an extremely dangerous set of behaviors that will eventually consume the family's energy and resources if not defeated. The best way to stop a bad habit is to replace it with a positive habit. Read the following list and determine which positive actions your child, with the support of the family, can begin taking today.

Accept the support of others who care

Admit to your abuse and talk about it with your parents and counselor

Agree to drug screening

Attend religious services

Commit to recovery

Consider the future

Cooperate with family counseling

Develop a plan for recovery

Develop a substance-free hobby

Draw

Encourage others to be substance-free

Follow the instructions of your doctor

Forgive the past

Get a chemical dependence evaluation

Get counseling

Hang out with substance-free friends

Help others

Identify temptations for relapse

Improve school attendance

Improve school grades

Join a school-sponsored club

Join a support group

Keep a journal

Know the facts about addiction and substance abuse

Learn anger management

Listen to the concerns of others

Play a sport

Read recovery literature

Sign a contract for substance free living

Verbalize the destructive nature of chemical dependence

Work out or exercise

Write your addiction story

Write your recovery story

Add several antidotes of your own:

_____   _____

_____   _____

_____   _____

_____   _____

_____   _____

Identify several of your danger zones or temptations for relapse and choose an antidote that will help you keep your commitment to remain substance-free.

Problem	**Antidote**
Examples:	*Examples:*
• My old friends that drink and use drugs invite me to a party.	• I decide to do something with my substance-free friends instead.
• I am tempted to skip school and get high.	• I talk to my counselor and commit to improve my attendance one day at a time.

Problem	Antidote
• _____	• _____
• _____	• _____
• _____	• _____
• _____	• _____
• _____	• _____
• _____	• _____
• _____	• _____
• _____	• _____
• _____	• _____
• _____	• _____
• _____	• _____

My most helpful strategy is: _____

The person I can turn to for support is: _____

The biggest reason I want to continue my recovery is: _____

_____

Name: _____

Date: _____

OUR COMMITMENT TO A SUBSTANCE-FREE LIFESTYLE

GOALS OF THE EXERCISE

1. Commit to abstaining from substance usage.
2. Identify a personal support system.
3. Commit to seeking intervention and therapy when there are signs of a relapse.
4. Support the child's plan for long-term abstinence from mind-altering substances.

ADDITIONAL HOMEWORK THAT MAY BE APPLICABLE TO SUBSTANCE ABUSE ISSUES

ADDITIONAL PROBLEMS THIS EXERCISE MAY BE MOST USEFUL FOR

- Abusive Parenting
- Prenatal Parenting Preparation
- Sexual Responsibility
- Strategies for Teenagers
- Suicide Prevention

SUGGESTIONS FOR USING THIS EXERCISE WITH FAMILIES

In the "Our Contract for A Substance-Free Lifestyle" activity the parents and the child are asked to sign a contract committing to abstinence from mind-altering substances, and to successfully contact supportive people or agencies in the event of any signs of a relapse. The contract worksheet reminds the child and the parents that there are many supportive people and agencies willing to provide time, encouragement, and resources to help with the difficult stages of recovery. However, recovery cannot begin without a committed intention to refrain from using addictive substances.

Both the child and the parents are asked to sign the contract as an indication of their commitment to supporting a substance-free lifestyle. Although a refusal to sign the contract indicates a desire for continued substance abuse, a signed contract does not guarantee abstinence without relapse. The contract is only an initial step in the fight against addiction.

OUR COMMITMENT TO A SUBSTANCE-FREE LIFESTYLE

INSTRUCTIONS FOR THE PARENTS AND THE CHILD

Personal control over substance abuse begins with a strong commitment to abstain from the use of any form of mind-altering substances. However, the child confronting substance abuse is not alone. Parents and other family members who care and are deeply invested in supporting the child's substance-free lifestyle are an essential resource in the fight for recovery. The contract below is a strong committment made by the child to remain free of chemical dependence and by the parents to support this commitment, by arranging for therapeutic intervention whenever they observe signs of a relapse.

Fill out and sign the following contract to commit to maintaining a substance-free lifestyle.

CONTRACT FOR A SUBSTANCE-FREE LIFESTYLE

I, _____, agree that I will not use mind-altering substances of any nature.

I, _____, further agree that if and when I sense any danger of a relapse or desire to use a restricted substance, I will successfully contact at least one of the people listed below to help me resist the temptation and honor my commitment to remain substance-free.

I understand that should my parents or any significant other suspect that I am in danger of a relapse, it is their obligation to contact my counselor or therapist immediately.

Signed: _____ _____
　　　　　　　　　　Child　　　　　　　　　　　　　　　　　　　　Parent

Signed: _____ _____
　　　　　　　　　　Counselor　　　　　　　　　　　　　　　　　　Parent

Date: _____

Individuals or agencies to call for help and support:

Mother: _____   Home: _____ Work: _____

Father: _____   Home: _____ Work: _____

Therapist: _____   Work: _____ Other: _____

Counselor: _____   Work: _____ Other: _____

Substance Abuse Hot Line: _____   Phone: _____

Emergency Room: _____   Phone: _____

Police or Sheriff: _____   Phone: _____

Supportive Other: _____   Home: _____ Work: _____

Supportive Other: _____   Home: _____ Work: _____

Supportive Other: _____   Home: _____ Work: _____

Section XXXI

SUICIDE PREVENTION

HEART-TO-HEART SMART TALKS

GOALS OF THE EXERCISE

1. Schedule regular appointments for parent/child communication.
2. Learn rules for effective communication.
3. Maintain a supportive and loving parent/child relationship.
4. Parents and children gain a better understanding of one another's point of view.

ADDITIONAL HOMEWORK THAT MAY BE APPLICABLE TO PARENT/CHILD COMMUNICATION

• Blended Family	Healing Hurt Feelings	Page 49
• Strategies for Children (Ages 7 to 12)	The Rewind Game	Page 315
• Strategies for Teenagers (Ages 13 to 18)	Listening with Empathy	Page 330
• Substance Abuse	Healthy Habits to Support Recovery	Page 343

ADDITIONAL PROBLEMS THIS EXERCISE MAY BE MOST USEFUL FOR

- Attention-seeking Behavior
- Blended Family
- Strategies for Children
- Strategies for Teenagers
- Substance Abuse

SUGGESTIONS FOR USING THIS EXERCISE WITH FAMILIES

Children who are depressed or who are in other critically volatile emotional states often stop communicating with their parents and others at a time when they vitally need the love and support of those who care. The communication that does take place frequently ends in heated differences, lack of understanding, and extreme frustration. The "Heart-to-Heart Smart Talks" activity emphasizes the importance of effective communication for both parents and the child. It leads the parent and child through the process of making time for productive and supportive emotional expression on an ongoing basis.

HEART-TO-HEART SMART TALKS

INSTRUCTIONS FOR THE PARENTS AND THE CHILD

Communication is a key element in any parent/child relationship. Effective communication becomes vital during emotionally volatile times of personal or family crisis. The expression of personal feelings, and listening non-judgmentally and with empathy, is one of the greatest gifts that parents and children can give to one another. Reserving a regular time for sharing feelings, concerns, ideas, plans, hopes, and dreams will strengthen the relationship and will develop a loving support system that enhances self-esteem and reduces anxiety and depression for both the parent and the child.

A "Heart-to-Heart Smart Talk" is an arranged conversation in which positive communication techniques are used to ensure that both parties feel they have expressed their ideas and that their points of view have been heard.

The rules for "Heart-to-Heart Smart Talks" are:

1. Select a time to talk privately that is convenient for both the parent and the child.

2. Any topic is okay to bring up.

3. It is okay to say "pass" or "not right now" when a topic becomes too uncomfortable.

4. Use active listening (i.e., listen non-judgmentally and with empathy).

5. Use I-messages (e.g., "I feel ..." "when ..." "because ...") as a way to express feelings and reactions without blaming the other person.

6. The purpose of a "Heart-to-Heart Smart Talk" is to understand the other person better, and not to try to give advice or change behavior.

7. Before concluding, agree on a mutually acceptable time for your next "Heart-to-Heart Smart Talk."

Below is a list of typical times that children and their parents can get together for a "Heart-to-Heart Smart Talk." Read over the list and add some additional time slots of your own.

After dinner	Breakfast	Scheduled appointment
After school	Dinner	Sharing a soft drink
After work	Family meetings	Shopping
Before bedtime	In the car	Taking a walk
Before school	Lunch	Working together

Additional times from the parent(s):   Additional times from the child:

_____   _____

_____   _____

_____   _____

_____   _____

Now respond to some considerations that will help you prepare for your next "Heart-to-Heart Smart Talk."

Active listening means that I will:

Parent's response: _____

_____

Child's response: _____

_____

Keys to expressing my opinion are:

Parent's response: _____

_____

Child's response: _____

_____

Some concerns my child has are:

Parent's response: _____

_____

Some concerns my parents have are:

Child's response: _____

_____

Some concerns I have are:

Parent's response: _____

_____

Some concerns I have are:

Child's response: _____

_____

Scheduled time for the next "Heart-to-Heart Smart Talk:" _____

Child's signature: _____

Parent's signature: _____

Date: _____

Appendix

ALTERNATE ASSIGNMENTS FOR PRESENTING PROBLEMS

Attention-seeking Behavior

Blended Family

Bonding/Attachment Issues

Career Preparation

Character Development

Children with Physical Challenges

Conduct Disorder/Delinquent Behavior

Dependent Children/Overprotective Parent

Depression

Divorce/Separation

Grandparenting Strategies

Grief/Loss

Oppositional Defiant Disorder (ODD)

Peer Relationships/Influences

Posttraumatic Stress Disorder (PTSD)

Poverty-related Issues

Prenatal Parenting Preparation

School Adjustment Difficulties

Sexual Responsibility

Sibling Rivalry

Strategies for Teenagers (Ages 13 to 18)

Substance Abuse

Suicide Prevention

ABOUT THE CD-ROM

INTRODUCTION

This appendix provides you with information on the contents of the CD that accompanies this book. For the latest and greatest information, please refer to the ReadMe file located at the root of the CD.

SYSTEM REQUIREMENTS

- A computer with a processor running at 120 Mhz or faster
- At least 32 MB of total RAM installed on your computer; for best performance, we recommend at least 64 MB
- A CD-ROM drive

Note: Many popular word processing programs are capable of reading Microsoft Word files. However, users should be aware that a slight amount of formatting might be lost when using a program other than Microsoft Word.

USING THE CD WITH WINDOWS

To install the items from the CD to your hard drive, follow these steps:

1. Insert the CD into your computer's CD-ROM drive.
2. The CD-ROM interface will appear. The interface provides a simple point-and-click way to explore the contents of the CD.

If the opening screen of the CD-ROM does not appear automatically, follow these steps to access the CD:

1. Click the Start button on the left end of the taskbar and then choose Run from the menu that pops up.
2. In the dialog box that appears, type **d:\setup.exe.** (If your CD-ROM drive is not drive d, fill in the appropriate letter in place of *d*.) This brings up the CD interface described in the preceding set of steps.

USING THE CD WITH A MAC

1. Insert the CD into your computer's CD-ROM drive.
2. The CD-ROM icon appears on your desktop, double-click the icon.
3. Double-click the Start icon.
4. The CD-ROM interface will appear. The interface provides a simple point-and-click way to explore the contents of the CD.

WHAT'S ON THE CD

The following sections provide a summary of the software and other materials you'll find on the CD.

Content

Includes all 60 homework assignments from the book in Word format. Homework assignments can be customized, printed out, and distributed to parent and child clients in an effort to extend the therapeutic process outside of the office. All documentation is included in the folder named "Content."

Applications

The following applications are on the CD:

Microsoft Word Viewer

Windows Only. Microsoft Word Viewer is a freeware viewer that allows you to view, but not edit, most Microsoft Word files. Certain features of Microsoft Word documents may not display as expected from within Word Viewer.

OpenOffice.org

OpenOffice.org is a free multi-platform office productivity suite. It is similar to Microsoft Office or Lotus SmartSuite, but OpenOffice.org is absolutely free. It includes Word Processing, Spreadsheet, Presentation, and Drawing applications that enable you to create professional documents, newsletters, reports, and presentations. It supports most file formats of other Office software. You should be able to edit and view any files created with other Office solutions.

Shareware programs are fully functional, trial versions of copyrighted programs. If you like particular programs, register with their authors for a nominal fee and receive licenses, enhanced versions, and technical support.

Freeware programs are copyrighted games, applications, and utilities that are free for personal use. Unlike shareware, these programs do not require a fee or provide technical support.

GNU software is governed by its own license, which is included inside the folder of the GNU product. See the GNU license for more details.

Trial, demo, or evaluation versions are usually limited either by time or functionality (such as being unable to save projects). Some trial versions are very sensitive to system date changes. If you alter your computer's date, the program will "time out" and no longer be functional.

USER ASSISTANCE

If you have trouble with the CD-ROM, please call the Wiley Product Technical Support phone number at (800) 762-2974. Outside the United States, call 1(317) 572-3994. You can also contact Wiley Product Technical Support at **http://www.wiley.com/techsupport**. John Wiley & Sons will provide technical support only for installation and other general quality control items. For technical support of the applications themselves, consult the program's vendor or author.

To place additional orders or to request information about other Wiley products, please call (800) 225-5945.

For information about the CD-ROM, see the **About the CD-ROM** section on pages 371–373.